Herbert Brown Ames

Canadian Political History

Herbert Brown Ames

Canadian Political History

ISBN/EAN: 9783337376369

Printed in Europe, USA, Canada, Australia, Japan

Cover: Foto ©ninafisch / pixelio.de

More available books at **www.hansebooks.com**

Canadian Political History.

OUTLINES

OF A

COURSE OF TEN LECTURES

DELIVERED IN CONNECTION WITH THE EDUCATIONAL WORK

OF THE

YOUNG MEN'S CHRISTIAN ASSOCIATION

OF MONTREAL

DURING THE AUTUMN OF 1894

BY

HERBERT B. AMES, B.A.

PUBLISHED BY THE
YOUNG MEN'S CHRISTIAN ASSOCIATION OF MONTREAL.
15 CENTS PER COPY.

CONTENTS.

INTRODUCTION.

The course of lectures, of which this pamphlet contains but the barest outline, was prepared and delivered, during the autumn of 1894, in connection with the educational work of the Young Men's Christian Association of Montreal. The object sought by the Educational Committee was to induce thinking young men of sound moral principle to take a deeper interest in Canadian national affairs. It was felt that for these to understand our system of government, to realize the sacrifices by which the present full measure of freedom had been obtained, and to appreciate the duties and privileges of citizenship, could not but result in the awakening of a deeper interest and in the exerting a stronger influence in favor of that righteousness which exalteth a nation. It is at the request of the students who attended the course that this pamphlet is published. As a means of refreshing the memory and for purposes of ready reference were these abstracts compiled. No literary merit is claimed for this production. Indeed, no such thought were possible where a lecture requiring an hour or more to deliver, required to be condensed into what might be read in ten minutes. Nor is any claim to originality put forward. The facts are taken from what are considered reliable sources. If challenged, the case must be argued with the original authors. At the end of several abstracts, a short bibliography is given, in the hope that many may be constrained to make further research and put flesh upon the bare skeleton of the outline. Canada has yet before her much of the work of nation building, and the larger the number of skilled workmen, since all must build whether or no, the more sound and sightly will be the construction.

H. B. AMES.

Montreal, Jan. 4, 1894.

LECTURE I.

THE OLD FRENCH REGIME IN CANADA.

Champlain's Government—System of Louis XIV—Governor and Intendant—The Superior Council—Feudal Tenure—Roman Catholic Church—Political Condition of French Canada prior to the Conquest—Treaty of Paris.

In order to clearly understand the spirit and estimate the influence of early French occupation in this portion of the North American continent, it will be necessary for us carefully to distinguish between such facts as are of mere romantic interest and those which have direct bearing upon the political history of Canada. To those who may desire to study the narrative of historic events more fully than we shall be able to do, let me recommend the lines that are followed by Francis Parkman, the historian, in the volumes of his work upon this subject. The divisions are somewhat roughly made. In some instances the chronology overlaps, but the following outline will give a fair, connected idea of the main characteristics and general boundaries of the different periods of the early French era :—

1. Discovery and early settlement, 1535 to 1635, vide " Pioneers of France in the New World."

2. The rise and fall of the Jesuit missions, 1635 to 1675, vide " Jesuits in North America."

3. The struggle for existence against the Iroquois, 1658 to 1701, vide " La Salle and the Discovery of the Great West," and " Frontenac and New France under Louis XIV."

4. Canadian feudalism, 1661 to 1760, vide " The Old Regime in Canada."

5. France vs. England in America, 1745 to 1760, vide " Montcalm and Wolfe."

But reading the works of Parkman, however fascinating, is hardly a study in Canadian political history. We must reluctantly turn from their narrative and devote ourselves to a consideration of such facts only as bear directly upon the purpose of our course.

The political history of Canada may be said to have commenced with the founding of Quebec by Champlain in 1608. The first form of government—that which he set up—was invested with large local authority. The governor was the centre of all power, and although assisted by a council, was not bound to follow its advice. Up to 1667 the history of New France contains little else than an account of the struggle for bare existence against the inroads of the Iroquois, and the severity of the surroundings.

System of Louis XIV.

With the accession of Louis XIV. to the throne of France in 1660, an entire change came over the policy of that country with regard to her colonial affairs. This king was the embodiment of the monarchical idea, and he determined to establish in America a reproduction of the provincial system as it had been brought to perfection by Cardinal Richelieu. The powers of the governor as they

Governor and Intendant.

had been exercised by Champlain, were now greatly curtailed, and the government of Canada brought directly under the control of the King himself. The Governor still held nominal power. He was military chief of the colony, and represented the Crown on State occasions ; but yoked with him was an officer known as the Intendant, usually of humble birth, but trained in the law and in administration. Without the consent of the Intendant, no public money could be expended, no regulation enacted, no transgressor brought to justice. In fact, the King of France, while not wishing to have these two colonial authorities quarrel, intended to have each act as a spy upon the other, and thus secure a critical report from two sources with regard to the minutest details of the administra-

The Superior Council.

tion. The Superior Council was also established at Quebec. It included the military governor and the legal-minded intendant, together with the religious bishop. There were also councillors appointed (not elected) by the King for life, varying in number from five to twelve. In this council was centred all legislative, executive and judicial power. Its members were responsible not to the people, but alone to the King. The people had no voice whatever in the management even of their purely local affairs, and public meetings were so effectively discouraged, as soon to cease altogether.

Feudal Tenure.

The system of feudal tenure was adopted in the disposal of all land. The greater part of Canada was divided into large estates and conferred upon seigneurs (usually men of noble lineage and modest fortune) in return for their doing homage to the King of France, and undertaking to colonize their respective grants. The seigneur in his turn conferred portions of his land upon "consitaires," on condition of clearing the same and the payment of certain dues to the seigneur. Since the Governor maintained the right, seeing that all land originally was conferred by grant of the King, to intervene at any time, in the King's name, and annul any arrangement between the seigneur and his vassal, it will be seen that the power of the former was of a nature both indefinite and uncertain.

From earliest times we find the Roman Catholic Church exercising Roman Catholic Church. a dominant influence upon all affairs of state. All land, as it was settled, was divided into parishes for ecclesiastical purposes, these divisions being afterwards recognized in the administration of local affairs. In each parish the influential men were the cure, the seigneur and the local captain of militia. Of these three, the representative of the Church carried the most weight in the community. Quoting from their own historians (" Doutre et Lareau," page 308) the position of French Canada up to the time of the British conquest, may be described thus :—

"Without education, without an opportunity of taking part in Political Condition of French Canada prior to the Conquest. public affairs, without an interest in the public offices, all of which were filled by persons sent out by the government, the Canadian people were obliged to seek in the clearing of the forest, in the cultivation of the field, in the chase and in adventure, the means of livelihood, and never busied themselves with public matters. Sometimes they thought they were becoming " a people " on this continent, and might acquire a larger degree of liberty, but all such aspirations were promptly checked by the Governor, the intendant, and the bishop, in obedience to the instructions of the King. No social union existed between the people, no guarantees of civil liberty were ever established. On every occasion the people were taught to have no ambition for civil power, or have a share in public business. Reduced at last to a state of passive obedience, they accepted the orders and edicts of the King without murmur."

On Sept. 8, 1760, the terms of a capitulation, by which Canada The Treaty of Paris. became a British possession, were signed. Full religious liberty was granted the French-Canadians, and certain religious bodies allowed to retain possession of their goods and privileges. The subsequent Treaty of Paris, signed on Feb 10, 1763, transferred to Great Britain all of the former possessions of France in North America, except St. Pierre and Miquelon, unimportant islands in the Gulf of St. Lawrence.

Before considering the system of government that was conferred upon French Canada upon the taking possession of that country by the British Crown, it will be well for us to turn aside and refresh our memory with regard to British institutions. Old French Canada was like a sturdy trunk, upon which was engrafted a new civilization. In order to rightly estimate the result, one must understand the nature, not only of the trunk but of the graft as well.

LECTURE II.

THE BRITISH CONSTITUTION.

Early Anglo-Saxon Ideas—The Norman Conquest and the Feudal System—
The Great Council—Magna Charta—Origin of Houses of Lords and Commons—
Parliaments of Edward I—Supremacy of Parliament—Bill of Rights.

Inasmuch as the British form of government served, to a very great extent, as the model for that of the Dominion of Canada, it is well at this point to spend a little time considering it. We will not undertake so much to describe the features of the present governmental system, as the principles which underlie them. By the term "Constitution," we mean the system under which a country is governed. The British Constitution came into existence at no particular date, its origin being shrouded in obscurity, and it has been gradually amended to suit the necessities of the time. Great Britain differs from most of the Continental nations, in that the Roman occupation left no perceptible influence upon its political institutions. The Saxon invader had escaped Romanizing influences.

Early Anglo-Saxon Ideas. The three leading Anglo-Saxon ideas were an elective king, with executive but not legislative powers ; a representative council of free men : and an established principle that no man should be taxed without his own consent. The Witan, or representative meeting of wise men, named the king and could depose him. By its authority laws were made and taxes imposed, it being the king's duty to carry out these decrees. No important act could be committed without the Witan's consent.

Norman Conquest. With the conquest of England by William the Conqueror, 1066, came a temporary submersion of the Saxon ideas of popular liberties. William introduced the Feudal System, upon the principle that the soil was the absolute property of the Crown. The land was parcelled out among his chief men upon condition that they were loyal to him and attended him in time of war with armed retainers. These chief men in turn distributed the land among vassals, every vassal being bound to defend and obey his lord. In **Great Council.** place of the Witan, we now find the Great Council of the nation, but it differed from the Witan in that it was not a representative body, being composed only of feudal barons who had been created through the King's gift of land. It took many years for the old Saxon ideas to work up through the Norman system, this being possible only because of the tenacity with which the people clung to the common law of the land and the principles of government that had prevailed in the time of Edward the Confessor. From time to time the Great Council was called together by the King to vote him moneys. It never lost this opportunity to effect a bargain for the abolition of some abuse, or the granting of some concession.

With the Magna Charta, 1215, is ushered in the age of written Magna Charta. legislation. The Great Charter, however, did not create liberties ; it merely recognized officially what had previously existed. It established, in writing, that no man should be imprisoned, or in any way brought to ruin, save by legal judgment of his peers ; and also that no tax should be imposed except with the consent of the Council of the realm. The constitution of the Council was also regulated, it being agreed that all Archbishops, Bishops, Abbots, Earls, and greater Barons should be summoned to it by the King's letters. Gradually the precedent was established that any to whom a writ of summons had once been issued by the King, might claim for himself, and his eldest son after him, the right to attend this Great Council, and out of it finally grew the House of Lords.

It must be remembered, however, that there was nothing repre-Origin of Lords and sentative about the Great Council of King John's time. This ele-Commons.' ment was added later. The gradual growth of small towns, that no longer needed protection of a feudal lord, brought about the establishment of a number of independent communities. For consent to collect revenue from these communities, it was necessary for the King to grant them representation. Hence we find that, by the middle of the 13th century, it was found necessary to summon to the Great Council citizens and burgesses and knights of the shire, elected from the free-holders themselves ; and in the reign of Henry III., in the year 1265, we find Simon de Montfort issuing writs directing the election of two knights for each county, two citizens for every city, and two burgesses for every borough, to serve in the Great Council of the kingdom. Thus began the elective assembly, which later separated itself into the House of Commons.

In the reign of Edward I., was passed the famous statute that no Parliaments of Edward I. tax should be levied except with the joint consent of the Lords and Commons. The parliaments that Edward I. gathered at the end of his reign, are identical with those that sit to-day. From this time on, King, Lords, Commons, Courts of Justice, the forms of public administration, our local provisions and provincial jurisdictions, the relations of church and state, in great measure the framework of society itself, had taken the shape which they essentially now retain. By the reign of Edward III. we find the "commonalty" fully acknowledged as one of the estates of the realm. Some time afterwards the Lords and Commons became separate bodies. To-day the taxation of the country is entirely regulated from the House of Commons. There had been little legislation prior to the time of Edward I. All the struggles had been for the observation of the old laws. With the perfected parliament of Edward I., 1295, commences a time of legislative activity. England had assimilated all that was assimilatable in the Norman ideas, and the old principles of liberty emerged from Norman domination. For a long time, however, the status of the Commons was an inferior one. It was understood that they might only petition, and that the King with the advice and consent of the Lords, assented and enacted. Oftentimes these enactments were by no means what the Commons had asked for. By virtue of their petitioning powers, the Commons were at first critics merely, and could initiate no legislation.

Supremacy of Parliament.

The next three hundred years after the reigns of the Edwards, was a struggle for supremacy between the King and the parliaments. There was law enough, but the kings repeatedly attempted to escape every constitutional fetter, to reign without parliamentary authority, to impose taxes by their own authority, or to legislate with the consent only of their own council. Parliament, with varying success, endeavored to hold the monarchs to the strict letter of the law as understood in the time of Edward I. Sometimes parliaments were packed or subservient, and the kings assumed extraordinary powers. Parliament assembled only at irregular intervals, being called together when the King wanted money, and being dissolved by the King when it in return demanded what he did not choose to grant. Under such conditions as these passed the periods of the Wars of the Roses, of the Houses of Lancaster York and Tudor. But with the House of Stuart and the arbitrary rule of James I. and Charles I., we find Parliament again vigorously asserting itself. This was the beginning of the end of the final struggle between personal monarchy and parliamentary government. The parliament of King James established the precedent that it had the right to discuss any question relating to the public good, whether the King had asked its opinion or not. The early parliaments of Charles I. maintained the right to demand the dismissal of unpopular royal advisers. The story of Charles' continuous quarrels with his various parliaments is not necessary here. Revolution was the result, and the King lost his life. When in 1689 parliament abandoned James II. and offered the joint sovereignty to William of Orange and Mary, it meant that the ultimate decision in the state was transferred from the King to the parliament. The 15th century had seen the power of the Lords predominating in the state ; the 17th closed with the power of the House of Commons predominating.

The Habeas Corpus Act of 1679, established that any person im- Bill of Rights. prisoned was entitled to be brought into open court and learn the nature of the charge against him, and if shown to have been improperly detained, should be set at liberty. When William and Mary ascended the throne, the Bill of Rights established the authority of parliament and confirmed the freedom of the subject. This date, 1689, may be considered the commencement of modern English history, inasmuch as the two hundred years that have since passed, have been occupied merely in developing the unwritten constitution. This famous Bill of Rights declares : (1) That a King cannot override existing laws. (2) That no money can be levied without a grant of parliament. (3) That any subject has the right to petition His Majesty. (4) That the size of the standing army shall be regulated by parliament. (5) That the election of members of parliament shall be fair and free. (6) That statements made in parliament shall be unquestionable in court. (7) That parliament shall be held at regular and frequent intervals. 8) That the revenues of the Crown shall be voted annually by parliament. (9) That judges shall be hereafter responsible to parliament and not to the King.

The development of government by party comes in at about this period, and William has the credit of being the author of the idea of Cabinet government. With the Bill of Rights, the British Constitution may be considered as evolved, and we now understand the authority that enacted a system of government for Canada in 1774, and the principles which Englishmen wished to have established in British North America.

Vide- Green—"A short history of the English People."
Albany de Fonblanque—"How we are Governed."
C. H. Wyatt—"The English Citizen."
H. D. Trail—"Central Government."
Oscar Browning—"The Citizen, his Rights and Responsibilities. '

LECTURE III.

THE CONSTITUTION AND GOVERNMENT OF THE UNITED STATES.

Periods of American Political History—The American System in its Legislative, Judicial and Executive Departments—State and Local Governments—A Comparison between some Features in the American and Canadian Systems—Influence upon Canadian Constitution.

At the same time that Great Britain was gaining control over the northern portion of this continent, she was loosing her grasp upon the central and southern sections. To the south of Canada a new nation sprung into being in a decade, a nation that was to evolve from British ideas a purely democratic form of government, and promulgate a constitution that has been considered by many the foundation for an ideal republic.

Some knowledge of the form of government adopted by this newborn nation, and of what experience taught regarding its adaptability to meet the needs of succeeding years, is necessary for the student of Canadian political history, since the American example and experience both left a deep impress upon the Canadian constitution.

Periods of American Political History.

We have hardly space to more than outline the periods of American political history. The student, by parallel reading, must develop these ideas for himself.

Briefly reviewed, the political history of the United States—from the granting of the charters by James I. to the Plymouth and London Trading Companies, to the constitutional amendments as a result of the war of the Secession—shows as its chief divisions the following :—

The period of Colonization...................... 1607-1750
The period of Expansion........................ 1750-1763
The Union of the Colonies...................... 1763-1775
The War of Independence........................ 1775-1783
The Evolution of a National Government........ 1777-1789
The Development of the United States under the Constitution. 1790-1850
Tendencies to disunion and the Civil War........ 1850-1865
The reconstructed nation........................ 1865-date

This chapter, however, must be devoted more especially to the two following lines of thought :—

(1.) A consideration of the system of government in vogue in the United States to-day.

(2.) A comparison between some features in the American and Canadian systems,—wherein we think our method superior to theirs.

The government of the United States is a federation which is the most complicated form of government known to civilized communities. Its essence lies in the fact that in every part of the country two governments and two sovereignties rule. There is a complete central government with certain powers over the States which comprise the federation, while each separate State is supreme over its own affairs within certain limits. The United States then, to-day, is a republic, itself composed of forty-five republics. According to the constitution, the functions of the National Government fall under three departments,—legislative, judicial, executive. These departments are co-ordinate, acting as far as possible independent of one another. It is the legislative department that enacts the laws, the judicial which interprets them, and the executive that enforces the laws after they have been made and interpreted. The Legislative Department consists of a Congress in which there are two bodies, the Senate and the House of Representatives. The Senate represents the States as States, each State, whether large or small, sending two members. The House of Representatives represents the citizens of the nation. Senators are elected by the Legislatures of the several States for a term of six years, one-third being renewed every two years. the Vice-President is the chairman of the Senate. Its work is largely done by standing committees. Its Legislative functions are exercised together with the House of Representatives. It has, however, also judicial functions, such as the trial of impeachments, and executive functions, such as the approval of Presidential appointments and the ratifying of treaties. The House of Representatives is renewed in toto every two years. The present House contains three hundred and sixty-five members, or about one to every 175,000 inhabitants. The House is too large to admit of much debate, hence its work is largely done by committees. Says Prof. Bryce, "It rules through and by its committees, and the whole House does little more than register by its votes the conclusions which the committees submit. One subject alone, taxation and appropriation, receives genuine discussion by the House at large." There are about sixty committees. Laws are made by joint action of Senate and House. The signature of the President is also required. If this be refused, a bill can become a law without Presidential approval, by a two-thirds vote of both Houses. If the Senate and the House disagree

The American System.

Legislative Department.

and both insist, a compromise is usually effected by means of a joint committee.

Judicial Department. The Judicial Department, as we have said, interprets and applies the laws which the nation has made. It consists of one Supreme Court, nine Circuit Courts, and sixty-four District Courts. Its jurisdiction extends only to questions arising in regard to the Federal laws, questions between States, etc. The United States laws are the Federal Constitution, the Federal Statutes and Treaties, the State Constitutions, and the State Statutes. In case of conflict between them, they rank in importance in the order named.

The Executive Department. The Executive Department applies and enforces laws as enacted and interpreted. The President is the chief executive officer. He is elected once in four years by means of the Electoral College. His chief duty is to see that the laws of the nation are faithfully executed, to act as commander of the Army and Navy, to represent the nation in foreign affairs, to appoint all officers of the Federal Government, and he may from time to time recommend certain courses of action to Congress by means of a Message. The executive functions of the Federal Government are committed to nine departments and three commissions. The heads of eight of the most important departments form the President's Cabinet, are appointed by him, and are responsible to him alone. Each department is divided into bureaus, each bureau into divisions, each division into rooms.

State and Local Governments. The nation performs only such functions of government as relate to the collective interests of the people. All other functions are performed by the State. The States are divided into administrative divisions,—counties, townships, cities and towns. Each State has its own Constitution, its executive, consisting of Governor and officials ; its Legislature, made up of Senate and Assembly; its system of local government and of State and local taxation, its State debt, its body of private law, its courts without federal appeal, and the qualification for citizenship differs with the States. Of all this, however, we cannot further speak.

Comparison between features of American and Canadian systems. In closing, let us consider a few of the weaknesses in the American system, which the framers of the Canadian constitution have sought to avoid. (1.) In the United States, each State regulates all matters not specially handed over to the National Government. In Canada, the National Government controls all matters not specially mentioned as belonging to the Provinces. The "residuum of power," as it is called, rests, with us, in the nation, with them, in the State. Our tendency is towards a strong, and theirs towards a weak, central power. The American Civil War, the railway strike of last summer, are examples of the disadvantages arising out of this principle. (2.) The American Senate represents a collection of States considered equally important. Rhode Island and New York have each two senators. The American Senate can act contrary to the wish of the majority of the people. This was evidenced in the dead-lock over the Sherman Bill, and recent tariff legislation. The Canadian Senate recognizes the greater interest of the larger provinces, and it would be hardly possible for the Canadian Senate to represent a minority. (3.) The American President, once elected, passes out of the reach of popular opinion. For four years he can be removed only in case of violation of the constitution. Within a year or two of his election, it may be possible, in fact is at present the case, that his policy is quite contrary to that of the majority of the people, and yet he must continue to the end of his administration. Not so with the Canadian Premier. He can lead only so long as confident that he represents the will of the majority. The moment he feels this confidence is lost, he must make way for another who has it. (4.) Any representative may introduce into the American House a bill interfering with the revenue. If it become law, it rests with the administration to provide the funds. With us such measures can only be introduced by the ministers who cannot be, contrary to their wish, compelled to assume further obligations. (5.) The American executive is independent of the Legislature. The members of the Cabinet, so-called, cannot in person explain or defend the conduct of their departments upon the floor of Congress. In Canada, the heads of administrative departments are Cabinet Ministers in the true sense of the word, and have seats in the House. They can explain and defend their actions. If their management of affairs becomes unpopular, the adverse criticism of their confreres can cause them to resign. (6.) In many American States there are elective judges. Sometimes these remain in office but for a comparatively short time. This does not remove them from political influence, and they are not as liable to be impartial as when appointed, as in Canada, by the Crown for life. 7. The American Speaker is chosen by the dominant party, and has very large power, since he has the nominating of the members of the several committees, and since, too, no one can address the House unless the Speaker "recognizes" him. The Canadian Speaker, though also elected from the party in power, has no such wide privileges in the naming of committees.

Between 1774—when a system of government was first granted British North America by Parliament—and 1867—when the Canadian Constitution extant to-day was drawn up—this nation to the south of us, having formulated a constitution of her own had been able to put it to sufficient test to demonstrate to our legislators *Influence upon the Canadian Constitution.*

wherein lay its good and its bad features. The British system, it is true, is fundamentally the Canadian model, but this model has been materially altered, owing largely to the American example and experience, and therefore some idea of the American system was necessary for an adequate appreciation of our own.

Vide—C. D. Higby—"Outline of Civil Government."
Prof. Bryce—"The American Commonwealth."
Encyclopædia Britannica.

LECTURE IV.

HOW THE CANADIAN CONSTITUTION WAS DEVELOPED.

The Five Periods—Canada a Royal Colony—The Quebec Act—The Constitutional Act—Development of Representative Institutions—The Union Act—Growth of Responsible Government—How Confederation came about—Passage of the B. N. A. Act—Canada a Part of the British Empire.

We are now prepared, having considered the condition of Canada prior to the conquest, the nature of the super-imposed British institutions, and the career and example of the neighboring republic, to take up the study of the development of our own Canadian constitution.

The Five Periods. To this end let us divide the political history of Canada into five periods :—

(1.) The old French regime, 1608-1760;

(2.) Canada as a colony under the direct control of Great Britain, 1760-1791.

(3.) The development of representative institutions, 1791-1840;

(4.) The growth of responsible government, 1840-1867.

(5.) The Confederated Dominion, 1867 to date.

Canada a Royal Colony. Of the first of these periods we treated in our first chapter, wherein we ascertained that the French-Canadians at the time of the conquest were without the semblance of popular government.

On the first day of February, 1763, the Treaty of Paris was signed.

This treaty guaranteed to the French Canadians the free exercise of their religion, but did not definitely establish whether the old laws of the country or those of Great Britain should obtain. That same year, by proclamation of George III., a system of government was set up, and Gen. Murray appointed Governor. He was to make laws with the advice and consent of a council appointed by himself, and an assembly elected by the freeholders ; but before the popular representatives could take their seats in the assembly, it was obligatory that they should take the oath of allegiance and supremacy, and make a declaration against transubstantiation. As the people were all Catholics, and no Catholic could conscientiously make this declaration, no representative ever appeared to claim his seat. The government was consequently carried on solely by the Governor and his Executive Council. The revenues of the country were at the disposal of the Crown, and might be used both for local purposes and Imperial defences. The people might levy direct taxes upon themselves for local improvements if they so desired.

In 1774 the British Parliament granted to Canada a definite sys- The Quebec tem of government with a constitution, by an Act known as the Act. Quebec Act. In order to conciliate the French Catholics, whose allegiance it was feared the American Revolution might shake, large liberties were granted them. Notwithstanding opposition on the part of the English who had taken up residence in British North America, the French civil procedure in matters relative to property and civil rights was authorized, whilst the criminal law of England supplanted any previous code. The hated test oath was abolished. but with it was also withdrawn the offer of an elective assembly. Lord Dorchester, the first Governor under this constitution, carried on the government by means of a Legislative Council of twenty-three members nominated by himself. One-third of this Council were Roman Catholics, but they did not sit as representatives of the people, nor were they in sufficient number to greatly influence legislation in favor of their countrymen.

At the time of the Conquest, Canada contained 65,000 souls, The French and Roman Catholic almost to a man. When the Ameri- Constitutional can colonies revolted, some 40,000 United Empire Loyalists emi- Act. grated to British North America. Of these, 10,000 established themselves in what is now Ontario. By 1790 the total population of the British American colonies had reached 165,000 souls. There now became a clashing of interests between the English and French speaking portions of Canada, the French having the majority in one. the English in the other. To end this was passed the Constitutional Act, 1791, making two provinces, and giving to each a representative form of government, made up of an appointed Council and an elective Assembly, with powers to make laws. Parliament still

2

reserved the right to determine how the Canadas should raise revenue, but left the disposal of the same to the local Legislatures. All public officials were appointed by the representative of the Crown. The two governments now organized, met for the first time in 1792, that of Lower Canada at Quebec, that of Upper Canada at Niagara. Each Legislature was opened by a Lieut.-Governor, and adopted as far as practicable the rules and procedure of the British Parliament.

Development of Representative Institutions.   For nearly thirty years, political affairs in each Province proceeded with a fair degree of harmony. Gradually friction developed between the appointed Council and officials on the one hand, and the representative Assembly on the other. The struggle was fought over the questions of money and patronage. There were certain revenues not controlled by the representative branch. The executive took advantage of this to govern without the Assembly. Not being able to starve the executive into submission, the people's representatives could not hold the officials to responsibility for the rightful performance of their duties. It became almost a matter of indifference to the executive as to whether their actions were pleasing or otherwise to the representative body. Every office with salary attached, from Prime Minister to Sergeant-at-Arms, was in the gift of the Governor, and filled usually with his imported friends. In fact, the system granted by the Constitutional Act of 1791, was a strange mixture of representative government coupled with an irresponsible executive. The same struggle was in progress in Nova Scotia, Prince Edward Island and New Brunswick. The difficulty was first settled in New Brunswick, 1836, and from the time that all revenues were placed at the disposal of the representative branch of the Legislature, we find there no further lack of harmony. In the Canadas, discontent grew more apparent until it culminated in the Rebellion of 1837-8. Although this was quickly quelled, it served to call to the notice of the Imperial Parliament the necessity of another change in the Canadian Constitution. Lord Durham was sent out as High Commissioner, with practically absolute powers, and his report and recommendations formed the foundation of the settlement that came about with the Union Act of 1840, and ushered in a new and liberal colonial policy, establishing a truly responsible government.

The Union Act.   Lord Durham's report recommended the union of Upper and Lower Canada into one province, with equal representation in one common legislature, and that this legislature be entrusted with responsible government. As a result, a bill was drawn up upon these lines, and after receiving consent of the colonists themselves, it passed Parliament in the summer of 1840,—this being the Union Act, before mentioned. This act provided for :—(1.) A Legislative Council of twenty members, and a Legislative Assembly of eighty-

four members, each of the former provinces to have equal representation ; (2.) This representation could be changed only by a two-
thirds' vote of both branches of the Legislature ; (3.) The English
language alone should be employed in Legislative records ; and (4.)
All revenues should go to make up a consolidated fund out of which
Civil Service salaries and other charges having been first paid, the
balance should be at the disposal of the Legislature. With the
control of the civil list by the elective Assembly, the executive was
thenceforth the servant and no longer the master of the situation.
From this time on, England appears to have been willing to remove Growth of
Responsible
all restrictions that were declared obnoxious by the Canadian Government.
people. Lord Sydenham was instructed to administer the government " according to the wishes of the people," and to summon to his
council those persons who had the confidence of the inhabitants.
Lord Elgin received instructions " to act generally upon the advice
of his Executive Council, and to receive as members of that body
those persons pointed out to him as possessing the confidence of
the Assembly." By 1850, the Canadas, Nova Scotia and New
Brunswick were in full possession of a system of self-government
such as their own public men had advocated. Between 1840 and
1867 the Canadian Legislature passed many important measures
which received Imperial assent :—(1.) The independence of Parliament was fully secured, and judges and officials debarred from sitting in either House. (2.) An elaborate system of municipal government was perfected, thus relieving the Legislatures from much
local legislation. (3.) The clergy reserves were divided among
various municipalities. (4.) Seigniorial tenure was abolished. (5.)
The Canadian Civil Service was put upon a business basis, and pre-
ference given to home talent.

The Imperial Parliament also passed several acts during this
period, relating to Canada :—(1.) It formally gave up all claim to
the right to dispose of provincial moneys. (2.) It granted to Canada
control of the Post-office service. (3.) It surrendered to Canada
the regulation of all matters relating to trade and commerce, so
that Canada has ever since arranged her tariff legislation. (4.) It
repealed the old navigation laws which hampered trade in the St.
Lawrence. (5.) It repealed the clause of the Union Act which refused to recognize the French language in Legislative records. (6.)
It authorized an elective Upper House.

The union between the Canadas lasted from 1840 to 1867, when How
Confederation
it gave place to the Federation we have to-day. It will be remem- came about.
bered that the Union Act provided that the two provinces, formed
into one, should each have equally representative powers. At that
time French Canada had a larger population by some 200,000 than
English Canada, and felt somewhat aggrieved at losing the addi-

tional representation to which it appeared entitled. But during the next twenty years, English immigration flowed rapidly into Upper Canada, so that by 1861 that province had 300,000 more people than had Quebec. It was not long before a demand came from the English province for increased representation. This demand the French province bitterly opposed as contrary to the terms set forth by the Union Act. The parties became so evenly balanced that it was almost impossible to carry on public business, until in 1864 there was a practical deadlock. The leaders of both parties then agreed, as the only way out of the difficulty, to endeavor to bring about a federal union of all the British North American provinces. It so happened that representatives of the Maritime Provinces were meeting at Charlottetown to discuss a similar proposition for a Maritime union. Eight members of the Canadian Ministry attended their meeting, proposed the new and larger scheme with such effect, that all the provinces agreed to send representatives to a further conference at Quebec, which was held on the 10th of Oct., 1864. Here a statement of seventy-two resolutions was drawn up, which formed the basis of the ultimate union. The delegates returned to their respective Assemblies to secure their ratification to the draft resolutions. The Canadian Legislature readily agreed. New Brunswick did not consent, however, until 1866, and Nova Scotia some time after. A final conference was then held in London, the whole ground again carefully gone over and a few minor alterations made in the interests of the Maritime Provinces. A bill was drawn up, known as the British North American Act, which passed the Imperial Parliament and received Royal assent on the 29th of March, 1867. This new constitution came into force on July 1, 1867, which date is the birthday of the Canadian Federation. The following year the great North-West was purchased, and in 1870 the Province of Manitoba was carved out and admitted to the Union. British Columbia also joined the Dominion in 1871, on the understanding that it should be connected with the Eastern seaboard by a line of railway. Prince Edward Island was the last to seek admission in 1873. Newfoundland, though originally represented in the Quebec Conference, still holds aloof, and its government is as distinct from that of the Dominion as is that of Australia or the Cape of Good Hope.

The British Empire to-day includes one-fifth of the land surface and more than one-fifth of the world's population. As a market for her manufactured products, this empire is of immense value, while England depends very largely for existence upon the supplies and raw materials of her colonies. It is recognized plainly in England to-day, that Canada is necessary to the unity of the Empire, and of all the Colonial possessions Canada enjoys the fullest pri-

21

vileges of self-government. The entire expense of defending the Empire is borne by Great Britain, Her protection prevents foreign attachment, her capital opens up Canadian industries, her sons have become our most acceptable colonists. Our only expense is the cost of Rideau Hall, which, since Confederation, has amounted to about three million dollars. England does not attempt to tax us ; on the contrary, she submits to our levying high protective duties upon her manufactures. While Canada has not the right to negotiate treaties in her own name, her right to be represented direct, in all negotiations affecting her, is conceded. The demand for exclusive control of our treaty making is hardly a fair one, unless we are ready to dispense with England's assistance in enforcing the provisions thus made.

Vide—Dr. J. G. Bourinot's "Manual of the Constitutional History of Canada;" "Local Government in Canada" and other works.

LECTURE V.

THE CANADIAN CONSTITUTION.

Textual Study of the British North America Act 1867, Sections 1 to 95.

Preamble—Divisions of the Act—Preliminary—Union—The Central Executive Power—The Central Legislative Authority—Provincial Constitutions—Provincial Legislative Authority—Distribution of Legislative Powers.

We have reviewed the steps leading up to the formation of the Canadian Confederation ; we have spent an evening each in the study of the British Constitution, and the American example ; now we will make a textual study of a portion of the Canadian Constitution as granted by the Imperial Parliament in 1867, and known as the "British North America Act."

The Act opens with a preamble which (1) sets forth the occasion for its enactment ; viz., that the Provinces of British North America have expressed a desire for union ; (2) defines the nature of this union to be federal and under the British Crown; Preamble.

(3) declares that the constitution to be given shall follow the British model ; (4)states that such union would advance both colonial and British interests ; (5) proceeds to define the scope of the ensuing Act, in that it shall provide for the establishment of Legislative authority and declare the nature of Executive Government, in the new Confederation ; (6) provides for future admissions into this Union ; and (7) closes with an enacting clause declaring the source from which the constitution emanates, viz.: the British Sovereign and Parliament.

Divisions of the Act.

The Act itself is separated into eleven divisions, as follows :—

1. Preliminary ; sections 1 to 2.
2. Union ; sections 3 to 8.
3. Executive power ; sections 9 to 16.
4. Legislative power ; sections 17 to 57.
5. Provincial constitutions ; sections 58 to 90.
6. Distribution of Legislative powers ; sections 91 to 95.
7. Judicature ; sections 96 to 101.
8. Revenues, debts, assets, taxation ; sections 102 to 126.
9. Miscellaneous provisions ; sections 127 to 144.
10. Intercolonial railway ; section 145.
11. Admission of other colonies ; sections 146 to 147.

Then follow five schedules defining the electoral districts, taking inventory of provincial stock-in-trade and assets, and giving formulae for oath of allegiance and declaration of qualification.

Preliminary.

The Preliminary Division gives the official name of the Act and provides that powers therein relegated to the Queen shall pass by inheritance to her successors.

Union.

The Division referring to the Union, sections 3 to 8, provides—for an official birthday for the Dominion (afterwards announced as July 1, 1867)—that the name "Canada" henceforth belong to the Dominion instead of only to a part thereof ; that Upper Canada be now known as "Ontario," and Lower Canada as "Quebec," and that the legislative union previously existent between them from 1840 to 1867, be severed, and each province hereafter have its local legislature, and that a decennial census shall, commencing with 1871, be hereafter taken, upon which shall be based the representation in Parliament of the various provinces.

The Central Executive Power.

The Third Division of the Act, Sections 9 to 16, undertakes to define the nature of the Executive Government. At its head is the British Sovereign, represented in Canada by the Governor-General. The Governor-General chooses and summons his advisers, and that body is known as the "Queen's Privy Council for Canada" (the "Cabinet" being the Executive of this Council). The powers formerly enjoyed by the several provincial governors, are now united in the Governor-General. The British Sovereign is declared to be the official head of the Canadian army and navy. The capital of the Dominion is fixed at Ottawa.

The Fourth Division of the Act, Sections 17 to 57, provides for the constitution of the Legislative authority in the Dominion. There shall be one general Parliament for the Dominion. This shall consist of three branches; viz.:—Queen, Senate, and House of Commons. Parliament shall be assembled within six months of the union, and thereafter meet at least once a year. The privileges, immunities, and powers of members shall be as in Great Britain. The number of members in the Senate as stated in the Act is 72. (It now numbers 81.) Originally the three divisions Ontario, Quebec, and the Maritime Provinces considered together, had equal representation. The qualification for Senators then follows. Their appointment is made by the Governor-General. The Queen has further power in emergency to name three or six additional senators. (A power never as yet called into use.) A senator's tenure of office is for life. He may, however, resign, or, under certain conditions enumerated, may cease to be qualified. The Governor-General appoints the Speaker of the Senate. Fifteen members form a quorum ; a majority decides, the Speaker always votes, and a tie vote is equivalent to a negative. The number of members in the House of Commons, as stated in the Act, is 181. (There are now 215.) The House is summoned by the Governor-General. No Senator can also be a member of the House. Then follows in the Act an enumeration of the electoral districts of the four provinces to be followed in the first election. Ontario is given 82 members (now 92), Quebec 65, Nova Scotia 19 (now 21), and New Brunswick 15 (now 16). The elections, until otherwise provided, should be held under the election laws of the several provinces. Provision is then made for the first election and for casual vacancies. (This election law has since been altered, as we will see in Lecture X.) The Speaker of the House shall be elected from and by the members of that body, and over it he shall preside. Provision is made in case of his absence, permanent or temporary. Twenty members form a quorum of the House, a majority decides, and the Speaker votes only in case of tie. The life of a House shall not exceed five years, though the Governor-General may earlier dissolve it. Quebec shall continue to have 65 representatives in the House. As 65 is to Quebec's population, so shall the representation of any given province be to its population, a readjustment of representation to be made after each decennial census. Sections 53 to 57 treat of money votes, and Royal assent. Measures dealing with revenue must emanate from the House, and only upon recommendation of the Governor-General. (This practically

The Central Legislative Authority.

means that they must come from the Ministry.) A bill having passed Parliament requires Royal assent. This may be either immediately granted by the Governor-General, acting in the Queen's name, or such assent may be withheld, or the bill may be reserved for further consideration by the Home Government. Any act may be disallowed by the Queen within two years, and cannot be in force as law without Royal assent.

Provincial Constitution. Division V. of the Act, sections 58 to 90, deals with provincial constitutions.

With the introduction of the British North America Act, 1867, we find the position previously occupied by the Imperial Government towards each separate colony now filled by the newly created Dominion Government. The colonies are now provinces. Where before Imperial control had been directly exercised over each, now this is superseded by Dominion control, and the Imperial Government is called upon to deal only with one central power. As there was now a division of authority between the central and local governments, it was necessary that such colonies, as previously had had governments of their own, should have the limits of their new powers defined ; and it was necessary that the old province of Canada, which by the Act was divided into two provinces, should be furnished with a local government for each of its new divisions.

The sections (from 58 to 90) of the British North America Act, 1867, which make up division V. of this Act, treat of the regulations affecting the Provincial Legislatures. Sections 58 to 68 deal with the Executive power, being nearly the same in each province. Sections 69 to 90 deal with the Legislative power, which varied considerably with the several provinces.

The chief executive officer of each province is the Lieut.-Governor. He represents the Dominion Government. His appointment emanates from the Governor-General in Council, to whom he is responsible, and by whom he may be removed. His term of office ordinarily is five years, his salary being provided for out of the Dominion funds, and his oath of office being similar to that of the Governor-General. In his capacity as chief executive, the Lieut.-Governor is advised by an Executive Council called together by himself, though responsible to the Legislature. The Lieut.-Governor may act contrary to the advice of his Council, but he does so at his peril. In the Province of Quebec, this Council to-day is composed of seven members, the Provincial Treasurership at this moment being vacant. In case of a Lieut.-Governor being unable to discharge his duties, a substitute may be appointed by the Governor-General-in-Council. The Act then fixes the capitals for the various provinces, expressly stating, however, that it remains within the power of the Local Legislatures to change the seat of government if so disposed.

Sections 69 to 90, next treat of the provincial legislative authority; Provincial Legislative Authority. and this consideration falls under six sub-divisions :—(1.) Provisions expressly applicable to Ontario, (sections 69 and 70); (2.) Specially applicable to Quebec, (71 to 80); (3.) To Ontario and Quebec, (81 to 87); (4.) To Nova Scotia and New Brunswick, (88); (5.) To all but New Brunswick, (89); (6.) Provisions alike applicable to all of the four provinces, (90).

(1.) The Ontario Legislature consists of a Lieut.-Governor and one House only, styled the Legislative Assembly. (New Brunswick, Manitoba, Prince Edward Island, and British Columbia have also but one House.) Formerly the Ontario House contained 82 members. There are now, however, 92, representing the parliamentary constituencies. Manhood suffrage, qualified by residence, obtains in Ontario.

(2.) Quebec has, besides a Lieut.-Governor, a bicameral legislature, that is, there are two Houses—a Legislative Council and a Legislative Assembly. The Quebec Legislative Council is composed of 24 members, appointed by the Lieut.-Governor for life. The districts they represent, their qualifications and the rules in regard to filling vacancies, are the same as in the case of Dominion Senators. The Council is itself the judge as regards what constitutes proper qualification of its members. One of their number is appointed Speaker by the Lieut.-Governor, ten members form a quorum, a majority decides, the Speaker always votes, and a tie vote is equivalent to a negative. The Quebec Legislative Assembly was, after Confederation, composed of 65 members. That number, in 1890, was increased to 72. The boundaries of the provincial electoral districts, therefore, no longer coincide with those made for Dominion purposes in this province.

(3.) Certain provisions now follow in the Act equally affecting both Ontario and Quebec. The first session of their Legislative Assemblies was directed to be held within six months of July 1, 1867. Each Lieut.-Governor was to summon in the Queen's name his respective Provincial Legislature. No official in the employ of the province could be also a member of the Legislative Assembly. It was understood, however, that this restriction should not affect members of the Executive Council. Contrary to American custom, a Canadian Cabinet Minister may sit in either House. A member, however, called to be a Cabinet Minister, requires to again come up for election in his constituency. The duration of a Provincial Legislature, unless it be sooner dissolved by the Lieut.-Governor, is four years, (in Quebec it has been altered to five years), and a period of one full year must not be allowed to elapse between the close of one session and the commencement of the next. The regulations regarding quorum, etc., which we have already considered in respect to the Dominion House of Commons, are practically the same for the Provincial Assemblies.

(4.) Nova Scotia and New Brunswick each had, at the time of Confederation, a properly constituted Legislature. It was provided that this continue under the same constitution as heretofore, except where the creation of the new power limited the former sphere of authority. The New Brunswick legislative body was actually in session at the time of Confederation, and this body was permitted to fill its limit of legislative existence.

(5.) The local Legislature of Nova Scotia, however, had fulfilled its time, and the new provinces of Ontario and Quebec had as yet no separate Legislatures. These three provinces, therefore, have provision made for them in the Act under which their first local elections were held.

(6.) In finally disposing of this subject of legislative power in the four provinces, provision is made in the Act that in matters relating to money votes and Royal assent, dealt with elsewhere from a Dominion standpoint, (see sections 55 to 57) the same procedure should be followed, mutatis mutandis, in Provincial Legislatures.

Distribution of Legislative Powers. And now coming to Division VI., we take up the consideration of that most important topic the Distribution of Legislative Powers. A sphere of action was to be provided by the British North America Act, 1867, for both the central and local authorities. Definite limits, within which each authority was to be supreme, must needs be set forth. It was to be settled at the outset where the Dominion and where the Province was to be in full control. The experience gained by the American republic, which had only just emerged from an exhaustive civil war over the question of States' rights, was to be so taken advantage of by Canadian law-makers, as to make the repetition of a similar catastrophe impossible upon Canadian soil. This Division VI., treating of the distribution of legislative powers, is made up of sections 91 to 95 of the Act. We will take up these sections seriatim.

Section 91 outlines the powers, in the matter of making laws, relegated to the Dominion Legislative. After making the general statement that Parliament may make laws " for the peace, order and good government " of Canada, on matters not expressly taken out of its hands and placed under exclusive control of the provinces, there follows for greater certainty a specific list of twenty-nine subjects, selected, as being so national in nature, as to rightfully fall within the control of the central power. This section closes with a declaration in effect that the " residuum of power " shall belong to Parliament and not to the Provincial Legislatures. Section 92, on the other hand, enumerated sixteen classes of subjects in respect of which the Provincial Legislature of each province may exclusively make laws. Thus, between the two lists, nearly every matter that can come up for consideration, is definitely assigned to one or other sphere of legislative authority.

Section 93 deals fully with the question of Education, laying down as a general principle the right of the Provincial Legislature to make laws upon this subject. But, owing to the fact that there was no system of national schools, but in certain provinces separate schools, wherein various denominations had, hitherto, according to their respective beliefs, determined what should be the instruction given their children ; and it was conceived to be not impossible that at some later date a majority in a Provincial Legislature might desire to override the wishes of the minority on these matters ; therefore, certain restrictions were laid upon provincial legislation, and the way left open for appeal to the higher power, should any parties have reason to feel aggrieved.

Section 94 gives to Parliament the right to legislate for three provinces, so as to bring about uniformity of laws in regard to property and civil rights, court procedure, etc. Any such legislation by Parliament would require, however, the subsequent approval of the local government before it could come into force as law in any province. Care is taken, however, in this section, to omit Quebec, wherein the French law, as it existed at the time of the cession, remains.

Section 95 deals with Agriculture and Immigration. Here we have a case of what is termed "concurrent powers." Each government may pass laws on these subjects. If, however, there is any collision, the Provincial Government is the one required to give way.

(To be continued.)

LECTURE VI.

THE CANADIAN CONSTITUTION.

TEXTUAL STUDY OF THE B. N. A. ACTS 1867–1886—*Concluded.*

The Canadian Judicature—Revenue, Debt, Assets, Taxation, etc.—Miscellaneous Provisions—Intercolonial Railway—Admission of Other Colonies—Final Schedules—Imperial Acts subsequent to 1867.

Judicature.

Division VII., the Judicature, is treated of in sections 96 to 101, inclusive. The Act provides for the appointment by the Governor-General, of Superior, District and County Judges in each province (except Probate Court Judges in Nova Scotia and New Brunswick). Until a uniform system of law prevails throughout the Dominion, judges of Provincial Courts shall be chosen from the bar of their respective provinces. This shall always be the case in Quebec. Superior Court Judges are appointed for life, being removable only by the Governor-General on joint address of Senate and House. Salaries of these judges are provided for out of the Dominion purse, being the seventh fixed charge upon the consolidated fund. The Canadian Parliament is given power, from time to time, to establish a Court of Appeal, and additional Courts as necessary. (This has since been done in the case of the Supreme Court of the Dominion.) Thus provision is made for the administration of justice.

Revenue, Debts, etc.

We have now reached Division VIII., comprising sections 102 to 126 inclusive, and dealing with Dominion revenues, debts, assets, taxation, etc. Parliament has full control of all Dominion moneys and revenues. These form one consolidated fund to be appropriated for the public service after the deduction of certain fixed charges. The first charge is the cost incidental to the collection of the revenue ; the second, the interest on the public debt ; third, the salary of the Governor-General ; then in order follows the payment of moneys borrowed to build the I. C. R., to purchase the North-West, borrowed for public works ; and the last fixed charge is the salary of the judges. These having been paid, Parliament can appropriate the balance as it desires. When Confederation was entered into, such assets of each province, as were readily convertible into funds, were credited to each province. Such public works as were of national utility were transferred from each province to the Dominion. All lands, mines, minerals, etc., still remained in the possession of the several provinces. The Dominion became liable for the previously contracted provincial debts, but as the proportional indebtedness of the provinces varied, the following plan was adopted. Ontario and Quebec were permitted to turn over to the new Dominion their united debt of 62½ millions. The Dominion further agreed to assume an eight million dollar debt for Nova Scotia and a seven million dollar debt for New Brunswick. The total net debt of the provinces, thus assumed at Confederation. amounted to about 75 millions. The building of the Intercolonial Railway and the C. P. R., of various public works, the purchase of the North-West, canals, waterways, etc., have gradually increased this amount, so that to-day the net debt of the Dominion is about 250 millions. As the Dominion had acquired most of the sources of provincial income, an allowance was made to each province to help pay the expenses of carrying on the local governments. Ontario was to receive (by section 118 of the Act), $80,000 per annum ; Quebec, $70,000 ; Nova Scotia, $60,000, and New Brunswick, $50,000; and an additional grant of 80 cents per head of the population. A further grant was also made to New Brunswick. After Confederation, all trade barriers between the provinces were removed. The products of one province were admitted free of duty into another. For a time, however, until one common tariff could be arranged, it was understood that where imported goods passed from one province into another, the difference between the two tariffs should be made good. For four years after Confederation, New Brunswick was allowed to collect her lumber dues. Dominion property and lands were declared exempt from local taxation. Such revenues as by this Act were reserved for the respective provinces, should be under the control of the Provincial Legislatures, each province having also its consolidated fund for the public service within its boundaries.

Division IX., which includes sections 127 to 144, contains a number of miscellaneous provisions :—Former members of Provincial Legislative Councils upon becoming Senators, should forfeit their old positions ; every member of the Senate or Commons, before taking his seat, should take the oath of allegiance and declaration of qualification ; until otherwise provided, the existing law-courts, officers, etc,. were to be continued; the former officials of the provinces were, in the main, to become employees of the Dominion, the Governor-General-in-Council having power from time to time to appoint such new officers as were needed. Section 132 explains Canada's position regarding treaties. As a nation, Canada cannot enter into treaties with another nation. Her treaties are made for her by the Imperial authorities. Canada has the right, however, to legislate as to how the obligations imposed by treaty shall be carried

Miscellaneous Provisions.

out. Section 133 states that either the French or the English language is permissible for all purposes in Parliament and in the Legislature of Quebec. The Provincial Lieut. Governors appoint their executive. It is with the advice and consent of this executive that the duties of each member of that body and of their subordinates are defined, and the Lieut.-Governor-in-Council appoints any further officers necessary, and defines their duties. This places the appointment of local officers in the control of the Provincial Government of the day. Then follow in the Act a number of provisions of a temporary nature, providing that, at the creation of the new central power, the previous acts and proclamations for Quebec and Ontario should be held to be valid until they were superseded by definite legislation. In settling the question of financial arrangements in the formation of the new Dominion, a Board of Arbitrators was named. A division of the records, formerly belonging to Upper and Lower Canada in common, was to be made by the Dominion Government. Power was also given the Lieut.-Governor of Quebec, to constitute townships in portions of the province hitherto unoccupied. The above outline of these miscellaneous provisions is necessarily very fragmentary and disconnected, as these sections were intended to provide for contingencies not stated in the main body of the Act.

Intercolonial Railway. Division X. One of the stipulations of the Union was, that a railway be built entirely upon Canadian soil, connecting the city of Quebec with the city of Halifax in Nova Scotia. This was undertaken by the Dominion Government, and has since been owned and operated by it. It is known as the Intercolonial Railway.

Admission of other Colonies. The last Division, XI., of the Act, provides that should the Canadian Parliament and the Legislature either of Newfoundland, Prince Edward Island, or British Columbia, petition the Queen for permission for one of these provinces to be joined to the union, such power would be granted by the Imperial Government. Newfoundland and Prince Edward Island were each to be entitled to a representation in the Senate of four members. The four members from Prince Edward Island, however, were to be deducted from those already assigned to the Maritime Provinces. At the end of the Act

Final Schedules. are five schedules :—The first gives the electoral districts for the first election after Confederation ; the second gives the twelve eastern townships, the boundaries of which were specially fixed under section 80 ; the third schedule describes the provincial public works and property that were to become the property of the Dominion, according to section 108 ; the fourth schedule gives a list of the assets in property which Ontario and Quebec conjointly contributed ; the fifth schedule gives the wording of the oath of allegiance and declaration of qualification required according to Sec. 28.

Since 1867 there have been four Acts that may rightly be includ- Acts subsequent ed in the Canadian Constitution :—The first is known as the Act to 1867. for authorizing a guarantee of interest on a loan to be raised by Canada to defray the expense of constructing the Intercolonial Railway. This we have seen to be the fourth fixed charge upon the Dominion revenue. Then in 1871 an Act was passed which provided for the establishment of new provinces not enumerated in the original Act, and made a fifth charge upon the consolidated fund by the purchase of the North-West. In 1875, a third Act was passed, removing certain doubts respecting Section 18 of the original Act, and making it possible for parliamentary committees to examine witnesses under oath, thus exceeding the privileges of Imperial committees. Finally, in 1886, a fourth Act was passed regulating the representation in Parliament which the territories, not included in any province, should have. These five enactments are known as the British North America Acts, 1867-1886. A copy can be readily obtained by sending ten cents to the Queen's Printer at Ottawa.

This necessarily imperfect outline covers the Imperial legislation which provided the Dominion of Canada with its constitution.

Vide -Clement's Canadian Constitution.
Munro—" The Constitution of Canada "
Houston—" Constitutional Documents of Canada. "

LECTURE VII.

THE DOMINION PARLIAMENT IN MOTION.

The Assembling of Parliament—The Opening Ceremonies –Queen's Speech—Committees—Method of Legislation—The Home of Parliament—How a Bill becomes a Law—The Permanent Departments.

We will suppose that there has recently been a general election, and that a new Parliament is about to assemble for its first session. The Governor-General, by proclamation in the Queen's name, summons the Senators and Commoners to appear upon a certain day at the Dominion capital for the despatch of public business. During the morning of this day, the members of Commons gather together in their chamber, take the oath prescribed in the British North America Act, and sign the roll kept by the clerk. At an appointed

The Opening Ceremonies.

hour in the afternoon, the Senate, whose Speaker has already been appointed by the Governor-General, assembles within its proper chamber. The Governor-General, escorted by military, and amid martial music and the boom of cannon, is driven to the entrance of the main Parliament building. He enters the Senate Chamber and occupies the throne. The Gentleman Usher of the Black Rod is now despatched to summon the Commons to attend and hear what the Governor-General has to say. This functionary, after rapping three times upon the door, enters the House of Commons, and in French and English summons its members to attend upon the Governor-General in the Senate Chamber. Upon arrival there, if the House has, as yet chosen no Speaker, its members are dismissed and told to reassemble the following day headed by a duly elected Speaker. Again assembling, the Governor General delivers from

Queen's Speech.

the throne what is known as the Queen's speech, which is supposd to declare the causes for the summoning of Parliament. This speech is, in reality, the composition of the Ministry, is largely congratulatory in character, and outlines only in the vaguest possible manner the proposed legislation of the session. After the delivery of the speech, the Commons retire to their own chamber, move a pro forma bill as a proof of their official existence, and then usually adjourn until the following day. It is customary for a resolution in reply to the Queen's speech, thanking the Governor-General for what he has said, to be moved and seconded in both Chambers. This is oftentimes the signal for the opening of a fierce party debate. The Opposition can hardly criticise the utterance of the Governor-General, but they frequently mercilessly handle the resolution in reply. If the Opposition feel strong enough, they may move an amendment, or even defeat the Government upon this first measure.

Committees.

One of the first proceedings of the session is the appointment of committees. This is usually done by a committee of selection, named by the Speaker. There are four kinds of committees :—(1.) The Committee of the whole House ; (2.) Standing or Permanent Committees, each named to consider a definite class of subjects ; (3.) Select committees, appointed from time to time for special business ; (4.) Joint committees, containing members of both Senate and House, for compromise purposes. There are in the House eight principal standing committees, those with which we are most familiar being, standing orders, privileges and elections, railway-canal-telegraph, private bills. These committees, as we shall see hereafter, play a very important part in the making of our laws.

The method of legislation is regulated, (1) by statutes, (2) by stand- *Method of Legislation.*
ing orders and rules, (3) by customs. Section 54 of the British
North America Act says that money bills need the Governor-General's recommendation, and section 133 requires all Acts to be printed
in both languages ; with these exceptions, the procedure of the
House is that of the English Parliament. There are three kinds
of bills :—Government bills, introduced by a minister with the consent of his colleagues ; public bills, introduced by a member, but
intended to enact laws affecting the whole people ; and private bills,
introduced by private members upon questions touching individual
citizens. Government bills are given precedence on government
days, and private bills on private members' days. Early in the
session it is customary for the Finance Minister to bring in the
" Budget," that is the annual financial statement. In connection
with this the estimated expenditure of Government for the coming
year is submitted to Parliament, and the members are asked to
vote the necessary funds. When the House becomes a Committee
of the Whole to consider the estimates in detail, it is said to be " in
supply." All measures for raising revenue to meet the expenses of
Government, are considered by the House in Committee of the
Whole, at which time the House is called the Committee of Ways
and Means. The introduction of the Budget and the request for
the necessary supplies, is usually made the occasion of an attack
upon the Government's entire policy by the Opposition, which being
pressed to a vote, tests the strength of the opposing parties in the
new House.

As we may now in imagination consider Parliament as duly con- *The Home of Parliament.*
stituted and in proper working order, let us visit the capital city
and view for ourselves the government machine in motion. Ottawa,
which was first occupied in 1865 as the capital of old Canada, is
situated between the Chaudiere Falls and the northern entrance to
the Rideau Canal. It is the centre of the lumber trade of the section. The main Parliament buildings are magnificently situated
upon a high bluff commanding an extensive view of the surrounding
country. The buildings are of cream colored sand-stone with red
facings, the architecture being twelfth century gothic. The central
tower rises to a height of 220 feet. The buildings cost about five
million dollars, and cover four acres. The chambers occupied by
the Senate and Commons are side by side. The Speaker in the
Senate Chamber is seated at the northern end, and the seats are arranged with a free space running lengthwise of the room. In the
Commons this method of arrangement is reversed, the Speaker being
seated upon the west side of the room, the members sitting at double
desks, the Government supporters upon his right, and the Opposition upon his left. The members of the Ministry, of whom there

3

are three in the Senate and fourteen in the House, occupy seats in the front rank, while the leading debaters of the Opposition sit in the seats nearest facing them. The visitor to the House, if fortunate enough to secure a copy of the orders of the day, finds that the routine proceedings are as follows :—(1.) Presenting petitions ; (2.) Reading and receiving petitions ; (3.) Presenting reports by Standing and Select Committees ; (4.) Motions ; (5.) Introduction of bills. Then come the orders of the day, questions to be put by members, notices of motion, etc. It is always of interest to the visitor to witness a division. The gong is heard throughout the corridors, and the members flock in to their seats. The Clerk of the House then rises and proceeds to call over the 215 names of the Assembly. If a member, when his name is called, desires to assent, he rises and bows. If he does not concur, he remains silent in his seat. The list is twice gone over, all the yeas answering the first time, and the nays, the second. The chief clerk then announces the result.

How a Bill becomes Law.

The successive stages by which a bill becomes law are of much interest. These are seven in number :—(1.) Introduction. In the House, every bill is introduced upon motion for leave specifying the title. The member having the bill in charge usually explains his measure, but there is at this point rarely any debate. (2.) Leave having been granted to introduce the bill, it is then read for the first time, without amendment or debate. The Speaker then proposes the formal question, " When shall the bill be read a second time ?" and a day having been fixed, its consideration is placed upon the orders of the day to come up in due course. (3.) Now comes the second reading, when the Commons discuss the principle but not the details of the measure. A vote is here usually taken and the bill may be altogether rejected. (4.) If, however, the principle involved is declared by the House to be a sound one, and the bill passes its second reading, it next comes to the Committee stage It may be considered by the House either as a Committee of the Whole, or may be referred to a Standing or Special Committee. Assuming the House to be in Committee of the Whole when the order of the day is reached, the Speaker puts the motion, " I do now leave the chair." Debate may here ensue. If the Speaker is permitted to leave the chair, the chairman of committees takes his place, and the bill comes up for consideration clause by clause. Changes may be made and amendments added. This is the critical stage of a bill. (5.) Having altered the bill to suit the majority of the House, the Committee of the Whole then rises, and the House is again properly constituted, and the previous chairman reports progress to the Speaker, relating what the House in Committee has done. (6.) It is then determined that upon a certain day the bill shall be read for its third and last time. No amendment is now expected. (7.) Finally, the motion is put " that this bill do pass," which usually carries, no one dissenting. The bill is now again printed, and goes up to the Senate, where it undergoes a similar course of treatment. If the Senate amend the bill, it must then be returned to the House to receive its concurrence. If the Senate pass the bill without amendment, however, it goes on to the Governor-General to receive the Royal assent. This having been given, the bill becomes law.

During the session, and while the Governor-General is in residence, the social life of Ottawa is exceedingly brilliant. When Parliament is prorogued, matters assume a very quiet aspect. There are, however, a number of permanent departments, the work of which goes on uninterruptedly during the entire year. These departments may be said to be thirteen in number, each being presided over by a Cabinet Minister and by a deputy head. The inferior appointments are made after civil service examination, the head of the department selecting whom he will from those duly qualified.

The Permanent Departments.

The following is a list of the departments :—

(1.) Trade and Commerce.—Presided over by the Premier, Sir Mackenzie Bowell, under whom are two sub-departments, that of Customs, over which N. Clarke Wallace. M.P., has control, and that of Inland Revenue, directed by J. F. Wood, M.P.

(2.) Justice.—Minister at its head, Sir Chas. Hibbert Tupper, assisted by Solicitor-General J. J. Curran, M.P. The Minister of Justice is the legal authority upon which the Crown and the various departments act. This department is responsible for the enforcement of law, the care of penitentiaries, etc.

(3.) State.—The Hon. A. R. Dickey. This department has control of state correspondence, records, registration, public printing, etc.

(4.) Finance.—Minister, The Hon. G. E. Foster. This department looks after the Dominion's financial transactions and superintends the Treasury Board and Audit Office.

(5.) Marine and Fisheries.—Presided over by the Hon. John Costigan, under whose charge are the lighthouses, pilots, ports, harbor commissions, signal service, etc.

(6.) Railways and Canals.—The Hon. John Haggart, which has control of the Government railways and canals, subsidized lines, tolls, etc.

(7.) Public Works.—The Hon. J. A. Ouimet, which manages the public buildings, harbors, dredging, etc.

(8.) Militia.—The Hon. J. C. Patterson, which looks after the Canadian militia and national defence.

(9.) Interior.—The Hon. T. M. Daly, controlling the Crown Lands,

Indian Affairs, North-West Territories, immigration, geological and natural history surveys.

(10.) Agriculture.—The Hon. A. R. Angers, which performs a variety of duties relating to agriculture, quarantine, statistics, archives, census, patents, copyrights, trade marks, etc.

(11.) Post Office.—Sir A. P. Caron directs the postal service of the Dominion.

(12.) Privy Council.—The president of which is the Hon. W. B. Ives. This is not an administrative department ; its main duty is to translate into workable rules the provisions of such laws as are made by Parliament. The President of the Privy Council is head of the Mounted Police.

(13.) Office of High Commissioner.—This office is held by Sir Chas. Tupper, who acts as resident agent for the Dominion at the Imperial Court in London.

The work of these departments makes a large force of employees necessary. The Ministers ordinarily spend most of their time directing their departments at the capital. No visitor should leave Ottawa without making the round of the immense departmental buildings.

Vide—Dr. Bourinot's Parliamentary Practice and Procedure in Canada.

The Statesman's Year Book, 1894.

The *Star* Almanac, 1895.

The Statistical Year Book of Canada, 1893.

LECTURE VIII.

CANADIAN POLITICAL PARTIES.

What is Party ? -Successive Canadian Ministries since 1867—The National Policy—General Election of 1887—Questions at issue in the Election of 1891—The Liberal Platform to date—Liberal-Conservative Platform for 1895—The Patrons of Industry—Prohibition—Protestant Protective Association—Parliamentary Independence.

What is Party?

" Party is organized public opinion, and this is at once its justification and the proof of its necessity. If any number of persons share a conviction, it is reasonable that they should unite to realize it." The political questions, affecting the Dominion, afford oppor-

37

tunity for wide divergence of opinion. The stand taken by our politicians naturally separates them into rival camps. Our purpose in this chapter is to ascertain and define the principles advocated by the various political groups which are to be found among Canadians.

We need scarcely revert historically to a date earlier than 1867. **Successive Canadian Ministries since 1867.** Prior to that time there had been it is true, Liberals and Conservatives, but Confederation was the work of the people irrespective of old time party opinion. The first ministry after Confederation, aimed to include the ablest representative men of both the former parties, and thus came into use the name of Liberal-Conservative. An Opposition party was developed from among those who had opposed the Confederation, afterwards augmented from time to time through other causes. There have been six Parliaments since Confederation, and soon the seventh shall have completed its allotted time. During this period five Ministries have held sway. On Nov. 6, 1873, the first Ministry resigned, and, upon an appeal to the country, the former Liberal opposition, under the Hon. Alexander Mackenzie, became the party in power. This administration continued during two Parliaments, covering nearly a space of five years. Since 1878 the Liberal-Conservative party has been in continued possession of a majority at Ottawa, and its leadership successively held by Sir John A. Macdonald, Sir J. J. C. Abbott, Sir John S. D. Thompson, and Sir Mackenzie Bowell.

Between 1867 and 1874, the Canadian tariff averaged only about **The National Policy.** 15 percent, and the country, owing largely no doubt to the effect of the American Civil War upon that Republic, enjoyed a full degree of prosperity. During the succeeding Liberal regime, the tariff remained about the same, being, if anything, slightly advanced. The Americans meanwhile adopted a high protective system which gained and preserved for them their home market. A time of depression now followed in Canada, and the Liberal-Conservatives began to urge an increase in the tariff, at first merely to raise additional revenue for developing the resources of the country, but afterwards with the purpose of affording incidental protection to home industries. On March 7, 1878, Sir John A. Macdonald brought forward the famous resolution in the House of Commons, setting forth the so-called National Policy. This resolution was defeated by the Liberal majority, but endorsed by the country at the succeeding election. It has been the main plank of the Liberal-Conservative party ever since. Another question causing party conflict in 1879, was the building of the C. P. R. During the first administration, a promise had been made to British Columbia that if she would enter the Confederation, which she did in 1871, a transcontinental railway would be undertaken by the Dominion Government. The

Liberals had not in the first place approved of this promise, nor did they while in power take any measures to put it into effect, but upon the return of the Liberal-Conservatives in 1878, immediate steps to redeem this pledge were undertaken. The road was completed in 1885, having cost nearly seventy millions of dollars. The question is still a debated one as to whether the advantages derived are commensurate with the expenditure thereby entailed.

General Election of 1887.

At the general elections in 1887, the two main arguments set forth by the Liberal-Conservatives for a continuance of public confidence were (1) the beneficial effects, already claimed to be apparent, as a result of the National Policy ; (2) the successful construction of the C. P. R. The majority of the Liberals strongly advocated free trade as the platform of their party. The Hon. Edward Blake, however, in his celebrated Malvern speech declared himself unable to see how the necessary revenue for carrying on the Government could be raised under free trade without resorting to direct taxation, and in consequence of this disagreement with the other leaders of his party, Mr. Blake resigned the leadership and was succeeded by the Hon. Wilfred Laurier.

The Election of 1891.

Coming now to the last general election, 1891, we will consider the opposing platforms in that contest. The McKinley tariff of 1890 was the direct occasion of the appeal being made to the electorate. Whether this Act was passed with hostile intent or not, it certainly did for a time cause hardship to certain Canadian producers. To secure some amelioration of its conditions became the avowed purpose of both political parties. Although the Government of Sir John A. Macdonald was entitled to another parliamentary session, this leader preferred dissolution, declaring as his reason that he desired to enter into negotiations with the American Government fresh from the electorate rather than with the support of a moribund Parliament. The platform of the Liberal-Conservative party, as set forth in Sir John A. Macdonald's last manifesto. issued on the 8th of Feb., 1891, may be summarized as follows :—(1.) The continuance of British connection ; (2.) A fair reciprocal trade arrangement with the United States ; (3.) A continuance of the National Policy ; (4.) The continued assistance to railways by liberal grants, and to steamship lines by generous subsidies, (the C. P. R. being cited as a proof of the success of this policy) ; (5.) No discrimination against Great Britain. The Liberals in reply argued (1.) That they too favored British connection, but if British connection clashed with Canadian interests, they were prepared to sacrifice the former rather than the latter ; (2.) They also favored reciprocal trade relations with the United States, being prepared to go much further in that direction than the Liberal-Conservatives; (3.) As to the National Policy. the Liberals would abolish every

vestige of protection in it. The country had not advanced, they
claimed, in consequence of this policy, but in spite of it. (4.) As to
the C. P. R., its enormous cost outweighed its advantages, and the
principle of bonuses and subsidies was bad, and they should be dis-
continued ; (5.) Although in favor of unrestricted reciprocity with
the United States, the Liberals stoutly affirmed that commercial
union was not necessarily a precursor of annexation.

The election of 1891 resulted in the continuance in power of the
Liberal-Conservative party. The Conservatives secured 125, and
the Liberals 90 seats in the new Parliament. While honors were
pretty evenly distributed in the central provinces, the Conservatives
were the greater gainers in the Maritime and North-West sections.
Since the general election, the Conservatives have strengthened
their position in the bye-elections, so that their normal majority in
the House to-day runs from 55 to 65.

Since the last general election, the Liberal party has somewhat ^{The Liberal}
remodelled its platform, and its views as set forth at the Liberal to date.
Convention held in Ottawa in June of 1893, are as follows :—(1.)
We favor a customs tariff not based upon the protective principle,
but upon the requirements of the public service ; (2.) We favor a
reciprocal trade arrangement with the United States whereby, in
return for gaining the American markets for natural products, we
are prepared to admit upon favorable terms a well-considered list
of American manufactured articles. (3.) We charge the party in
power with extravagance and corruption in its management and
expenditure of the public monies ; (4.) We stand for the strictest
economy in the administration of the Government, condemning
what we consider to have been the undue and unnecessary increase
in the public debt ; (5.) We demand that, hereafter, a Minister
accused of misconduct in office, be tried by the House of Commons,
and not by a partisan Royal Commission ; (6.) We demand that
the sales of Dominion public lands be made direct to settlers, upon
as reasonable terms as possible ; (7.) We demand that the provincial
franchise be adopted for Dominion elections ; (8.) We demand that
when electoral divisions are framed for the House of Commons,
the county boundaries be preserved ; (9.) We favor an elective
Senate ; (10.) We endorse the taking of a Dominion plebiscite in
order to ascertain the views of the people regarding prohibition.

At the approaching general election, the Liberal-Conservative Liberal-
party will stand pretty much by the old platform of 1891. The Conservative
Colonial Conference, held in Ottawa last June, with the prospect for 1895.
that it will encourage closer relations between the British colonies
and open further markets to the Canadian producer ; the trans-
Pacific cable and the trans-Atlantic service now in contemplation ;
the French treaty, recently ratified ; Canada's comparative immunity

during the recent world-wide period of financial depression ; the fact that a Democratic administration at Washington has considerably modified the severities of the McKinley tariff without it having been necessary for Canada to make sacrifices to obtain this end ; the measure of tariff reform that the Government carried through last session, and the modification of the Franchise and Banking Acts, liable to be accomplished during the coming session, all these will doubtless be urged by supporters of the present Government as additional reasons for their being granted a further lease of power. As the French say, " We shall see what we shall see."

The Patrons of Industry. And now we will consider the platform and principles of a new party, one not yet with separate representation within the walls of Parliament, and yet not probably long destined to remain unrepresented. I refer to the Patrons of Industry. This is primarily a farmers' organization. Its aim is to constitute a third party. Although the movement is now but three years old, it claims to have over one thousand associations and nearly 200,000 members in Ontario alone. The patrons have an independent delegation of 16 in the recently elected Ontario Legislature. They vehemently deny any affiliation with existing parties. Their platform is as follows : —(1.) Maintenance of British connection ; (2.) Reservation of the public lands for the actual settlers ; (3.) Purity of administration, and absolute independence of Parliament ; (4.) Rigid economy in every department of the public service ; (5.) Simplification of the laws and a general reduction in the machinery of Government ; (6.) The abolition of the Canadian Senate ; (7.) The election of county officials ; (8.) Tariff for revenue only, falling upon luxuries rather than upon necessaries ; (9.) Reciprocal trade upon fair and equitable terms between Canada and the world ; (10.) Legislation to protect labor and its products from combinations and monopolies ; (11.) Prohibition of bonuses and grants to railways ; (12.) Preparation of Dominion and Provincial voters' lists by municipal officers ; (13.) Conformity of electoral districts to county boundaries.

There is as yet no distinct Labor Party in Canadian politics. Probably the Patrons of Industry stand highest in favor with the militant electoral forces of organized labor.

Prohibition. The Prohibition Party has not, as yet, a separate existence in the Dominion House. Its ideas find acceptance with members upon both sides of the Speaker. It is probable that a majority of the electors in every province, with the exception possibly of Quebec, would vote, upon a plebiscite, in favor of prohibition. Such a measure can, however, only emanate from the Dominion Parliament, the Provinces having only the power to restrict the traffic. The main declaration of this party is as follows :—" That in their opinion the time has arrived when it is expedient to prohibit the manufacture, importation and sale of intoxicating liquor for beverage purposes." The Liberal party have introduced a plank in their platform for taking a Dominion plebiscite on this question. On the other hand, the Conservative party appointed a Royal Commission to consider the effects of the liquor traffic upon all interests, and the measures adopted elsewhere to lessen its evils. The recent manifesto of the Dominion Alliance strongly advocated a union of all prohibitionist voters for concerted political action, the putting forward of independent prohibition candidates in the various Parliamentary constituencies—or where this was unadvisable, the offer of the total prohibition vote to candidates of avowed prohibition principles—and the immediate organization for political work in every constituency.

Another organization, although hardly entitled to be included Protestant Protective among national political parties, "The Protestant Protective Asso-Association. ciation," requires mention. Its main purpose is to combat what it characterizes as "the aggressive efforts of the Roman Catholic Church to control the Dominion." It advocates a non-sectarian school system, the taxation of unoccupied religious properties, and considers the election of a Roman Catholic to office as perilous to national interests. The existence of this faction has tended to confuse the interests in more than one contest.

Probably the best known instance of independence upon the floor Parliamentary Independence. of Parliament is the secession from the Conservative ranks of Messrs. Dalton McCarthy and Colonel O'Brien. These gentlemen have supported the Conservative party in its general trade policy, but favor a greater measure of tariff reform than it has yet pleased the Government to introduce, while they condemn the gerrymander, the Caron whitewash, and would abolish the French language and separate schools outside of the Province of Quebec. Independents are not numerous in the Dominion Parliament. A member frequently finds a tender conscience to be a disadvantage rather than otherwise. There are probably not more than half-a-dozen on either side of the House who would desert their party from conscientious scruples.

Vide—Life of Sir John A. MacDonald.
Life of Hon. Alexander Mackenzie.

LECTURE IX.

CANADA'S FUTURE DESTINY.

The Possible Alternatives – Disunion of the Dominion—Annexation with the United States—From an American and from a Canadian Standpoint—Canadian Independence—Considerations in favor of and against Independence—Imperial Federation – Considered in the Canadian Parliament—Colonial Conference at Ottawa—An Imperial Parliament—Statement of Lecturer's conclusion.

When now we come to inquire what the future may have in store for this country, our first question naturally will be : " Does serious discontent exist with regard to the present situation ? " If the people of Canada are contented and happy, then we may infer that no change is imminent ; if, on the other hand, they are discontented and restless, we may expect to behold altered conditions in the near future.

In support of the contention that the former is the correct view of the case, let me point out the apparent lack of serious attention given to the consideration of the subject of this lecture : from which fact the conclusion is natural that this is not a burning question, else would it more frequently occupy the columns of our public prints, instead of serving almost wholly as a topic for literary articles or ornamental addresses. And why should not Canadians be content with existing conditions ? For the last fifty years Great Britain has kept back nothing in the way of self-government that our representatives have desired. We enjoy, to as full a measure, the advantages of British institutions as do the citizens of the mother land, and the limitations placed upon us are very slight. Yet there are some among us who are dissatisfied. These **The possible Alternatives.** declare for one or other of the following alternatives : disunion, annexation, independence, or Imperial federation. There are those **Disunion.** disunionists who, opposed to Confederatin at the outset, still consider it a failure. Their numbers are growing less with time. Another class, however, cherishing a somewhat similar idea, belongs to the present generation. These are the more Anglo-phobe of the French-Canadians in the Province of Quebec, who dream of an independent French-speaking republic upon the banks of the St. Lawrence. Sometimes they even contemplate a vast domain, French and Catholic, including Quebec and the New England States. Fortunately no French-Canadian of national influence supports this idea, the Hon. Wilfred Laurier having gone out of his way, upon several occasions, to declare against it. This dream is obviously unrealizable, as this province has not the resources requisite for an independent existence, nor would an exclusively French-Canadian management tend to make a prosperous community.

That there is a certain amount of sentiment both in the United States and Canada in favor of annexation, cannot be denied. As early as the time when the New England colonies separated from Great Britain, a provision was inserted in their constitution for the future admission of Canada. In 1849 a petition was signed by nearly a thousand leading citizens of Montreal, endorsing annexation and defining it as "a friendly and peaceable separation from British connection, and a union upon equitable terms with the great North American confederacy of Sovereign states." The idea has been formally recognized upon both sides of the line. As to the present attitude of the United States, as near as we can judge of it from the utterances of American public men, we would conclude that, while unwilling to make any half-way arrangement with Canada, the United States would admit the Dominion to a full share of the benefits and responsibilities of American citizenship. Certain American manufacturers, especially in New England are extremely anxious for the consummation of this project as destined to open a new market for their products. There are, however, other Americans who realize that the admission of Canada would be accompanied with many embarrassments. A Canadian unattached party would be suddenly interjected into American politics, the strong pro-British sentiment could not be expected to extinguish itself, and what to do with Quebec would be a problem. But, on the whole, we may regard America's desire to annex Canada as one of the dangers that beset us if we would continue to pursue our present way. Looked at from a Canadian point of view, it is claimed that annexation would bring great benefits to the Canadian farmer, lumberman, fisherman, and to some manufacturing industries. On the other hand it is pointed out that the United States is rather a competitor than a market for natural products, while, without increasing her industrial establishments, the United States could supply the markets of Canada with manufactured goods. As the New York "Sun" says, "In case of annexation, there is no competition across the border which we cannot crush out." Canada too, would have to assume her share in the responsibilities of American citizenship. To her own local problems would be added that of dealing with the freedmen of the South, the assimilation of America's enormous foreign immigration, the reconciliation of capital and labor, the silver question, movements like the Coxeyite

[margin notes: Annexation with the U.S. — From an American Standpoint — From a Canadian Standpoint]

march, and the struggle with gigantic American monopolies. It costs Canada five percent of her revenue to-day for defence purposes, while it costs the United States thirty-five percent. We would need to assume our proportionate share of this expense. The loss of identity, the blotting out of Canada from the map of the world, and the relinquishment of what it has taken a century to build up, would be a great grief to the majority of our Canadian people. For these reasons it is hardly probable that a majority will soon favor annexation. The French-Canadians, who enjoy peculiar privileges, would also probably strenuously oppose being swallowed up in the American Union.

Canadian Independence. Another idea, which has apparently taken deeper root in the hearts of the Canadian people than that previously considered, is that of Canadian Independence. This means a complete severance of the tie binding us with Great Britain, and the assumption, unaided, of all the duties and responsibilities of an independent nation. As an ideal of the far-distant future, we will not consider it, but will regard it, for purposes of discussion, as within consummation within our own generation. This idea, especially to our **In favor.** young men, is an exceedingly attractive one. The Hon. Wilfred Laurier has more than once expressed himself as awaiting independence. The Young Liberal Clubs, and, as a rule the Liberal press pronounce in its favor at no distant date. The latest utterance of importance upon this subject was the pamphlet issued by the Hon. Joseph Royal, ex-Lieut.-Governor of the North-West Territories, a Conservative, in the spring of the present year. By the advocates of Independence, it is claimed that Confederation has completed its work and must now make way for a new idea. As a colony, we can have no national spirit. Nothing short of independence can evoke the necessary sentiment required to unite all **Consideration against Independence.** the various elements. It is well, however, for us to consider whether we are likely to have to pay too dearly for this privilege. In the first place, would there be any advantage in replacing the Governor-General by a local politician ? Secondly, would our burdens of taxation be lightened or the reverse ? Our commerce is now protected throughout the world by the British flag. Were we independent, to accomplish this same end, it would be necessary to maintain an army and navy, fortifications and protected harbors, and a consular force at all the principal ports in the world. This could not but mean a vastly increased taxation. Then again, consider the position we would be in with reference to the United States. A country of five millions can hardly deal upon equal terms with a country of 75 millions. Past treatment has convinced us that we could not depend merely upon the innate sense of justice and humanity on the part of the United States. How did she treat

Mexico and Chili ? What would have been the result in the fisheries dispute and Behring Sea controversy had we been independent ? Does the contract labor law, the restrictive regulations on Canadian railways and discrimination regarding canals, assure us that we would be liberally treated by our more powerful neighbor ? It is the knowledge of our British connection alone that prevents annoyance from becoming aggression. Independence can mean nothing other than ultimate annexation. Our position outside the fold of Uncle Sam would soon become so intolerable, that whatever our scruples, we would be glad to form a part of his republic. It is well then for those who advocate independence to beware that they are not unwittingly helping on the cause of annexation. As to the French-Canadians, though many among them favor independence, the majority know when they are being well treated, and do not feel that they would enjoy any privileges in independent Canada, while they might lose some they already possess. It is hardly probable then that Canada, within the next fifty years will be prepared to cut loose from Great Britain and attempt to play the difficult role of an independent nation.

We will now take up the next alternative—Imperial Federation. _Imperial Federation._ Of this idea there are two phases—the moderate and the more advanced. The former proposition favors for the present, at least, a general closer relationship between Great Britain and her colonies, while the latter carries the idea farther, and formulates various schemes for a world-wide parliament of English-speaking peoples. As far back as 1861, we find Sir John A. Macdonald outlining a scheme for Imperial Federation as our ideal future. For the past ten years the Imperial Federation League, with headquarters at London and Toronto, have held periodic meetings and made considerable headway in the advancement of their ideas. From time _Considered in the Canadian Parliament._ to time, this question, in some form or other, comes up in the Canadian Parliament. In the spring of 1892, Mr. Alex. McNeill, member for North Bruce, introduced a motion declaring it to be the wish of the Canadian Parliament, whenever Great Britain saw fit to admit Canadian products into her markets upon more favorable terms than those accorded other nations, to accord corresponding advantages by reducing the duties upon British manufactured goods. In speaking to this motion, the Hon. Geo. E. Foster pointed out the difficulties, in the way of any step towards reciprocal trade relations, to be, from a Canadian point of view, the protective ideas of Canada and the necessary loss of revenue, and from a British point of view, the strength of the free trade sentiment in Great Britain, and the " most favored nation " clauses in existing British treaties. He did not, however, regard these difficulties as insurmountable. The Hon. Mr. Davies moved an amendment to the effect that Canada should reduce her duties upon British manufactured goods, without stipulating for benefits in return. This was lost, and the original motion carried by a vote of 97 to 63. This division shows with tolerable clearness the position of the Canadian Parliament on this question. Our present Government would be willing to enter into a give-and-receive arrangement with the mother-land, but not one which meant concession on our part only.

Colonial
Conference
at Ottawa.

The most important event of the past year, bearing on this idea, is undoubtedly the Colonial Conference, held in Ottawa last June. The Imperial Government was represented by the Earl of Jersey, and delegates were present from all the Australian Colonies, from New Zealand, and from the Cape. Among the resolutions approved were those advocating :—(1.) A Customs arrangement between Britain and her Colonies whereby trade within the Empire should be placed upon a more favorable footing than that which is carried on with foreign countries ; (2.) Until Britain could entertain for herself such a proposal as the above, the passing of such Imperial legislation as would enable the various colonies to enter without restraint into reciprocal trade relations with one another ; (3.) The removal of any clauses in existing treaties which prevent the self-governing colonies from entering into reciprocal trade arrangements ; (4.) The establishment of a trans-Pacific telegraph cable between Canada and Australia, and ultimately extending to the Cape, the expense of the survey to be borne equally by Great Britain, Canada and Australia ; and (5.) The approval of Canada's efforts to establish fast steamship communication on the Atlantic and Pacific, and the request that Great Britain grant assistance towards defraying the expense of the fast Atlantic service.

We have recently learned that Lord Jersey favorably reports to the Home Government upon the recommendations of this Conference. Any step taken by Great Britain along these lines would serve to cement the tie binding her with her colonies, and have a strong bearing upon the future of Canada. There are already ties of sentiment binding Canada with the mother-land, and it is likely that bonds of interest will be strengthened in the coming years. The British market consumes, in enormous quantities, just the products that Canada produces. The annual imports of food stuffs alone into Great Britain, amounts in value to nearly eight hundred million dollars per annum. Canada, during the last few years, has greatly increased her exports to Great Britain, while those to the United States are falling off. It seems probable that this increase will continue, and that, unless conditions materially change, Great Britain will become the chief market for Canada's agricultural products. This being the case, British connection will undoubtedly grow stronger.

The larger scheme of Imperial Federation contemplates an Im- An Imperial perial Parliament at London, in which representatives from all the Parliament. British possessions would have seats. While theoretically plausible, this plan, as yet, seems too advanced for present consideration.

In review, then, I would dismiss the idea of disunion without The Lecturer's comment as not being serious ; annexation, meaning absorption and Conclusion. obliteration, is, as yet, distasteful to the majority of Canadians, and, as long as this is so, cannot be our possible future ; independence, though a glorious dream for the far distant future, is impracticable for the Canada of to-day, and could mean nothing short of annexation ; the continuance of British connection, therefore, seems to me to be our probable future, and, as our relationship must needs grow closer or more distant as the years go by, I believe and hope that Canadians will accept the former alternative.

LECTURE X.

THE RIGHT OF DOMINION SUFFRAGE AND THE METHOD FOR EXERCISING THE SAME.

The Statutes regarding Elections—The Franchise Act—Who may Vote--How the Voters' Lists are Prepared and Revised—The Election Act—Issue of Election Writ—Method of Nomination--Of Election—Counting of Ballots - A Recount— Miscellaneors Provisions—The Controverted Election Act—Election Petitions.

We have now reached the final lecture of the course. Having considered the Government and institutions of Canada, it is requisite that we understand the methods provided whereby each citizen can make his influence felt in regard to these matters. We live under a popular form of government, and the will of the people is expressed through the ballot box. Art. 41 of the British North The Statutes regarding America Act provided that the Dominion Government in due course Elections might enact uniform election laws for the Dominion. So, when in 1883, the Parliament of Great Britain, after careful consideration of the entire subject, revised and strengthened the British statutes concerning corrupt and illegal practices ; taking this law and previous Canadian enactments as a basis, the Dominion Parliament passed three statutes in 1886, covering the entire subject of fran-

The Franchise Act.
chise and election procedure. These statutes are known as the Electoral Franchise Act (1886, R. S. C. 5); the Election Act (1886, R. S. C. 8), and the Controverted Election Act (1886, R. S. C. 9). Taking up the first of these, we ascertain who are entitled to vote in

Who may vote.
Dominion elections. Every person has a right to be registered upon the voters' list—for his own proper district—and when correctly registered has the right to vote, provided said person :—

(1.) Is a male.

(2.) Is of the full age of 21 years.

(3.) Is a British subject by birth or naturalization.

(4.) Is neither disqualified nor prevented from voting by any law of the Dominion.

These four qualifications are all prerequisite with every elector, but he must also be qualified as regards property or income, and as regards occupation or residence under one of the following conditions :—

(a.) Ownership. He must possess real property to the value of $300 in a city, $200 in a town, or $150 elsewhere ; and this ownership must have existed prior to the time of the revision of the voters' lists.

(b.) Tenancy. He must be the tenant of real property, under a lease, and pay a monthly rental of at least $2, a quarterly rental of at least $6, or an annual rental of $20 ; and shall have been in possession as tenant for the year next previous to his being placed upon the list.

(c.) Occupancy. He must be the bona fide occupant of real property worth $300 in a city, $200 in a town, or $150 elsewhere ; and this occupancy must have existed for one year next preceding his being placed upon the list.

(d.) Residence and income. This specially interests young men. One who derives an annual income of $300, that is, earns steadily $6 per week, and has resided in Canada for a year previous to the date of the revision, may thus qualify in the polling place where he resides at the time of the revision.

(e.) As a farmer's son. Such are qualified, provid'd the farm upon which they live with their father, is of sufficient value to give each a vote, as under the ownership clause, a year's previous residence being here also required.

(f.) As son of owner. This also interests our city young men. If a father, or in case he be dead, a mother, owns property of sufficient value if equally divided between parent and sons to give each the amount required under the ownership clause, then each may thus qualify to vote. Here, too, a year's previous residence is necessary.

(g.) As fisherman and owner. Such an one may qualify upon $150 worth of land, boats, fishing tackle, etc.

(h.) As annuitant, that is one who annually thus receives $100 per year, having resided within the district for a year prior to the revision.

Women, Chinamen and Indians west of Ontario, cannot vote.

The law provides for an annual revision, but the great cost which this would entail, is regarded as sufficient excuse for dispensing with this undertaking, except when Dominion elections are reasonably near at hand. An old list continues in force until replaced by a new one, and we sometimes have elections upon lists three or four years old. When a revision is determined upon, the Government appoints for each electoral district a person called the Revising Officer. In this province, he is usually an advocate or notary of at least five years' standing. The work of preparing a voters' list entails a preliminary and final revision. Early in June, taking for his basis the Dominion list in force, and comparing this with the latest municipal assessment rolls, and other available information, the revising officer undertakes the preliminary revision. He prepares two supplementary lists ; the former of names to be added, and the latter of names to be struck off. Any person claiming for himself or for another the right to be registered, may now appear and make proof. A solemn declaration is required, and if the proof be satisfactory, the name is added to the former supplementary list. The names of persons who are dead or no longer qualified, are placed upon the latter supplementary. These lists are open and on view for several months, the preliminary revision usually closing about Oct. 1. The original and supplementary lists are then printed at Ottawa, and returned to the Revising Officer. The lists are then exposed by being placarded in specified public places until the date of final revision, five weeks after such posting. Any person desiring, at the time of final revision, to have his name added to the list, must give notice to this effect to the Revising Officer ; and any person desiring to have names removed from the list must give similar notice also to the party objected to. On the day appointed, the Revising Officer holds his court of final revision and acts as judge upon all personal applications and objections. He adds or removes names as, according to the proof adduced, appears to him good and proper. The hearing concluded, the final list is prepared, the electoral districts divided into polling districts, each containing not over 300 electors, and a copy of the corrected list is sent to the Queen's Printer at Ottawa. Unless there be an appeal from the decision of the Revising Officer, the list as corrected, is final.

How the Voters' Lists are prepared and revised.

4

We will next consider the method of election as laid down in the Election Act and its amendments. While the British North America Act provides that not more than five years shall intervene between elections, they may take place more frequently at the desire of the Government. When a Government is overthrown or has decided to appeal to the country, the first official step is the issue of the election writs. These emanate from the Governor-General-in-Council, and are addressed to those chosen to act as returning officers, declaring it the will of the Sovereign that the Canadian Parliament be assembled upon a given date, and commanding the returning officers to cause elections to be held, naming the day of nomination. Upon receipt of a writ, each returning officer takes the oath of office, appoints his assistant, procures from the revising officer copies of the voters' list, and proceeds to select polling stations. At least eight days before nomination, the returning officer placards a proclamation stating the day of nomination, the day of election, where the polling stations are situated, and where the votes will be counted. Upon the day fixed for the nomination of candidates, between the hours of 12 and 2 the electors usually assemble, and the returning officer prepares to receive nominations. A nomination is made by the deposit with the returning officer of a properly drawn up and signed nomination paper. This document must bear the signature of at least 25 electors, must be accompanied with the consent in writing of the person nominated, and a deposit of $200, forfeitable in case the candidate receive less than one-half the number of votes cast for the person elected. Should more than one person be nominated, a poll is granted and the election follows one week later. The returning officer, as soon after the nomination as possible, causes notices to be placarded stating that a poll has been granted and that the choice lies between such and such candidates. A candidate may retire at any time previous to the closing of the poll. The returning officer now appoints a deputy returning officer for each electoral district, who in turn selects a poll-clerk. A certified list of voters for the polling district, a ballot box of approved pattern, the requisite quantity of ballot papers, and copies of printed directions for voters are furnished each deputy returning officer before he enters the poll. Every polling-booth must contain two apartments, the one to be occupied by the officers of the election, the other to enable the voter to mark his ballot in private. Each candidate is entitled to be represented within the poll by an agent commonly called a " scrutineer," who watches that no irregularities occur. The poll opens at 9 a.m., and the voting continues until 5 p.m. It is hardly necessary to describe the method of polling a vote. An elector, who is so desired by one of the scrutineers, must take the oath that he is qualified, and that he has not been paid or

The Election Act.

Issue of Election Writ.

Method of Nomination.

Method of Election.

51

promised anything for his vote. What constitutes a corrupt practise and the penalties attached upon conviction of the same, are all plainly set forth in the Act. At precisely 5 p.m. the poll is closed, Counting the Ballots. and the deputy returning officer, in the presence of the scrutineers, counts the ballots and gives each scrutineer a certificate stating the number of votes cast for each candidate, and the number of rejected ballots. The deputy returning officer then places in the ballot-box all papers and paraphernalia connected with the election, and locks and seals the box, which is transmitted to the returning officer, who makes an official count and summing up at the time and place specified in his proclamation. If no objection is made, the returning officer, six days later, transmits his return to the Clerk of the Crown in Chancery, who takes official cognizance of the same, and the candidate is duly proclaimed elected in the next issue of the Canada "Gazette." It sometimes happens that the defeated candidate or A Recount. one of his friends has doubts regarding the correctness of the result as declared. In such cases the statute permits of a recount upon certain conditions being complied with. This recount takes place before a judge, and may reverse a previous decision. The law pro- Miscellaneous Provisions. vides that all the candidate's expenditure be made through an authorized agent. Any bill for services connected with an election is outlawed if unpaid within one month. The agent is required within two months of an election to publish a detailed statement of all expenditures incurred in connection with the election, and any agent furnishing an untrue statement is guilty of a misdemeanor. This law if rigidly enforced, would do much towards preventing corruption in elections, but it is unfortunately, to a great extent, a dead letter.

A few words in closing, with regard to the Controverted Election The Controverted Act. After the result of an election has been announced, the de- Elections Act. feated candidate or his friends may feel that the seat has been un- Election Petition. fairly won, in which case the following method of recourse is open to them. An election petition is drawn up, signed by any elector, complaining that he has good reason to believe that the person, declared to be elected, was not duly returned, that another should have been returned in his place, or that the election should be void, or that corrupt practices have been committed. In this province such a petition is presented to the judge of the Superior Court, within forty days of the election, and the action is usually tried within the district where the election was held. The petitioner must deposit one thousand dollars to cover expenses. The trial takes place before a judge and not a jury. Witnesses can be forced to attend and testify and produce documents relevant to the case. The judge determines what evidence is permissible, makes his decision, and transmits the same to the Speaker of the House of Commons. Here also, an appeal lies from the ruling of the judge to the Supreme Court if the petitioner be dissatisfied. The Speaker, upon receiving the Judge's decision, gives the necessary directions to carry the determination into effect and reports to the House of Commons. An election petition may be withdrawn, though another elector may present himself and secure the substitution of his name to carry on the complaint. To withdraw a petition through any corrupt bargain or agreement, is an illegal act. Election petitions are usually numerous after an election, but by mutual consent the majority are withdrawn, and comparatively few come up for trial.

Thus have we very imperfectly attempted to outline the main provisions in the three acts which relate to the right of suffrage and the method of exercising the same. Every young Canadian should secure the registration of his name upon the voters' list for the division in which he lives, and regard his ballot as a most sacred trust to be used as a matter of conscience.

APPENDIX I.

A YOUNG MAN'S DUTY IN REFERENCE TO POLITICAL PARTIES.

(An Extract from Lecture VIII.)

"What should be a young man's attitude in reference to party politics?" We sometimes hear the dismal wail, "both political parties are hopelessly corrupt, no honest man can have his portion with either." It may be true that corruption is carried on under the cloak of both political parties, but we cannot believe that the forces of evil are dominant in either. Obviously the surest way to reinforce those evil influences and permit them to secure undisputed sway, is for good men to have nothing to do with either party and stand each upon his separate pinnacle, secure in his integrity. This is not, however, the advice I would give to young Canadians. If the good forces in each party seem to be battling against heavy odds, all the more reason why you, with your good intentions, should hurry to their reinforcement. For the moment, I care not to which political party you belong, but to one you certainly should own allegiance. Satisfy yourself, by means of careful investigation, as to which policy, followed out to its logical conclusion, would be likely to produce for Canada, the most beneficial results. Take a broad view, and do not be governed by local prejudices. Think for yourself, and be not content to receive your political principles, as you do your last name, from your paternal ancestor. If your political beliefs are really worth anything to you, they will deepen into convictions which should urge you on to aggressive action. Join the political party of your choice. Enroll your name with one of its working organizations. Throw yourself heartily into the work of spreading a knowledge of its principles, and aiding in every lawful manner its triumph at the polls. But always put principle first and party afterwards. Perhaps some day you may be asked by your party leaders to act contrary to the dictates of your conscience. What then?

This is the opportunity, which, such a man as you are, was created to seize. This is your chance to do the cause of pure government and your own party an inestimable service. We are presuming that the question at issue is not one of judgment, here you might do well to bend to the opinion of older and wiser men, but this is a question of principle, and you have only God and your own conscience to reckon with. That being the case, unflinchingly oppose the noxious project within the councils of your own party, and refrain from supporting it in action. You will likely hear some unpleasant things said, but in the long run you will have raised yourself in the estimation of your comrades and benefitted your cause. You may be even surprised to find that your political associates are still willing to accept your aid on future occasions. Only when it becomes evident that you are to be constantly at variance with your party, do I advise you to openly sever all connection with it.

Remember also, that a policy, however reasonable, if depending for its execution upon dishonest instruments, is sure to fail of good results. Unless there is a righteous man behind it, mere orthodoxy in party belief is of little value. However good the laws may be, dishonest men can use them for evil ends. If I were forced to choose between permitting the angel Gabriel to frame the laws, leaving it for Satan to enforce them, or vice versa, I should certainly say, let Satan do his worst at legislation, provided Gabriel had the interpretation and enforcement. And so if I had to choose between the bad nominee of a good party, or the good nominee of a bad party, I should certainly choose the latter as the lesser evil. If the party I usually endorse, makes a bad nomination, in the division where I have my vote, and the party I usually oppose puts forward a candidate spotless in contrast, I shall certainly vote against my party for its own good, but I will probably go into an adjoining constituency, where my party has done itself honor by a good nomination and there will I put in my heartiest work for both the policy and the man which I endorse. Such a course, followed by an electorate, would force both parties to make good nominations and give us more conscientious men in Parliament. It would give us a greater number of men willing to work loyally and earnestly for the party of their choice, so long as that party remained within the bounds of what was right, but who would not hesitate, when their party stooped to condone an evil, to declare black white, and wrong right, to unsparingly condemn such a course in caucus, and if there unable to make themselves felt, be willing to record their disapproval openly, by an adverse vote, upon the floor of the House. Ten such men could to-day change the face of Dominion legislation, could compel any party, desirous of securing or retaining power, to purge itself of such masures as were contrary to righteousness. I trust that the near future may see this dream realized.

Regarding Provincial Political Parties, there is, to my mind, little to be said. The well defined lines of political cleavage on national issues are well-nigh obliterated upon provincial questions. The main duty of a provincial government is to tax lightly, administer the revenue economically and honestly, and dispense even-handed justice to all classes in the community. Any government, whatever be the name by which it is known, which follows such a course, is worthy of support and any party which does not do this, should be promptly cast out.

As to our Provincial Legislature in the Province of Quebec, it really contains but two groups ; the one composed of those who will vote right from principle and the other of those who can be induced to vote wrong for a consideration. Our duty lies in distinguishing between these two classes, and extinguishing the latter, whatever be the party name by which its members are sheltered.

APPENDIX II.

THE CHRISTIAN YOUNG MAN IN POLITICS.

Being an Address delivered by Mr. Herbert B. Ames, B.A., before the Young Men's Christian Association of Montreal, February 19th, 1892.

The lack of interest evinced among our Christian young men, in regard to the national affairs of our country, has always been to me a cause for wonder and surprise.

How to account for this indifference, is a problem to which I have given no little thought and attention, but as yet without satisfactory result. Sometimes I think it is because our young men imagine that the country has no need of their services. This would imply either that the State is already perfectly governed and there can be no improvement : or else that such services , as our Christian young men can conscientiously render, are of no value. Neither of these suppositions seems admissable.

We have only to examine the true state of things either at Ottawa, Quebec, or in our own Civic Chambers. to be convinced that government has not reached such a stage of perfection nor politicians such an ideal of unselfishness, that it is wise to altogether dispense with the care and guidance of the Christian portion of our community.

The real cause of this lack of concern lies, I think, in the fact that our Christian young men are afraid of politics, as we understand the term. What little they do know of them is unsavory, and they feel that there is no place for them in the political arena of to-day, unless they are willing to stoop their colors and lower their principles. Hence, in the mind's eye of many a young man rises a vision similar to that portrayed by Dante in the Inferno. As over the door of hell appears the superscription "all hope abandon ye who enter here," so, over the door that opens before the Christian young man who has aspiration to enter public life or take some active part in citizenship, a similar inscription presents itself, "all righteousness abandon ye who enter here." I often measure up our public men by the somewhat old-fashioned, but yet never out of date standards that Moses, David, Jehoshaphat and the early Christian Church adopted. Listen to some of them :—Here is Jethro's advice to Moses :—" Moreover thou shalt provide out of all the people, able men, such as fear God, men of truth, hating covetousness; and place such over them, to be rulers of thousands, rulers of hundreds, rulers of fifties, and rulers of tens. And let them judge the people. . . ."—(Ex. xviii., 21-22.) These are some of the last words of King David :—" The God of Israel said, . . . He that ruleth over men must be just, ruling in the fear of God." (2 Sam. xxiii., 3.) And it was thus that King Jehoshaphat admonished his judges :—" Take heed what ye do, for ye judge not for man, but for the Lord, who is with you in the judgment. Wherefore, now let the fear of the Lord be upon you; take heed and do it; for there is no iniquity with the Lord our God, nor respect of persons, nor taking of gifts." (2 Chr. xix., 6-7.) And when the early Apostolic Church undertook to provide for the daily distribution, this was the advice upon which they acted :—" Choose out seven men of honest report, full of the Holy Ghost and wisdom, whom we may appoint over this business." (Acts vi., 3.)

I fear many of our public men will hardly show to advantage if estimated on such lines, but there are names upon which we can turn the search light of closest scrutiny and not fear to find what is dishonest or unclean. Some there are, worthy to be described as men " who never sold the truth to serve the hour,—nor paltered with eternal God for power."

Amid all the abuse of party warfare, no scandal has ever fastened itself to such as Gladstone and Garfield, Mackenzie and Blake, Mowat and Meredith, Thompson and Laurier, DeBoucherville and Joly de Lotbiniere. While these men live in the flesh or in the memory, it can never be said that politicians are universally corrupt. And should they be ? Is there anything inherently bad in what is known as politics ? Is it in nature and essence essentially

impure, and should it be polluting to those who come in contact
with it ?

If we consult our dictionary we find a dual definition for the word
politics.

1st. " Politics is the science of government. That part of ethics
which has to do with the regulation and government of a nation or
state, the preservation of its safety, peace and prosperity, the defence of its existence and rights against foreign control or conquest,
the augmentation of its strength and resources, and the protection
of its citizens in their rights with the preservation and improvement
of their morals."

This is politics as God intended it.

Surely the consideration of themes like these can have naught of
degradation in it. To spend life and energy in an honest endeavor
to bring about such results, should rather serve to elevate and en-
noble him who thus enlists. And is it not the duty of every man
to take this rightful place and fulfil the charge his Maker has laid
upon him ?

The state is but a whole made up of parts. Every citizen is an
integral part. The policy of the state is but the resultant of the
forces acting within it. You are one of those forces. Your individual force exerted goes to swell the resultant for good, or un-
exerted allows of a proportional increase to the powers of evil.

" He who is not for us is against us." He who is too indifferent
to exercise the duty of citizenship is not a neutral but a negative
force in the community. But I imagine I hear some saying : " All
this is theoretical, impractical. What are we to do with politics as
we find them ? We grant, that were politics as God intended them,
there would be an honorable place and activity for Christian men,
but what of politics in the sense in which the term is generally accepted and understood ? "

To treat this question with greater exactness, let me quote the
other portion of our double definition :—

" Politics is the management of a political party ; the conduct and
contests of parties with reference to political measures, or the administration of public affairs and the advancement of candidates
to office."

That is politics as man has made it. In this sphere you ask is
there any place for Christian young men.

We have now a serious question before us. As we do not desire
to understate the case, we must acknowledge that there exist many
grave evils in the conduct of politics understood on the lines laid
down above.

" Something is rotten in the state of Denmark," said Hamlet.
This may be as truly said to-day of the commonwealth of Canada.

I admit that there is much truth in the accusation that such is the management of political parties that a corrupt but energetic minority may rule an honest but lethargic majority, and endanger the very principles of representative government ; that our civil service, supposed to be conducted on business principles has degenerated into little better than a prize system by which services to the party in power are recognized and rewarded ; that so great has become the influence of money, that parties to win the elections deem it necessary to expend enormous sums, for the collection of which, begging, borrowing, bullying and even stealing is considered justifiable ; that no account is rendered to any responsible party, and that in the expenditure of this fund, the briber and the bribed, the rum-seller and the rum-drinker, the impersonator and the tough, all find employment and remuneration ; that in the United States nearly all respectable citizens are dropping out of public life ; that our country, our province and our city, while not having yet reached this pass, have not much to boast of, or grounds on which to make the assertion, " I am holier than thou."

I admit that in all this there is far too much truth, and I could go on enumerating what is at once too familiar and disgusting, were it not a waste of time, but here lies the main question :—Is there any remedy ?

In their revolutionary impatience, the Anarchists have avowed their hostility to all existing political forms except the free commune, which alone will be left standing among the general wreck they contemplate.

Sometimes when my blood boils at some fresh outrage on decency and good government, I feel almost tempted to cast in my lot with them and declare for a complete reorganization. But with human nature unchanged, little can be hoped for by methods so radical. What guarantee have we that the latter would be better than the former state ?

How often the question is asked : is it possible to dispense altogether with parties ; or unite the independent men of both camps to form a third that would restore politics and government to the pedestal of purity from which they have fallen ? Is it possible to dispense altogether with partyism ?

Party is organized opinion, and this is its justification and the proof of its necessity. If any number of persons share in a conviction, it is but reasonable that they unite to realize it. So long then, as there are common opinions, there must also be parties or aggregations of men united to support the propagation of these opinions. But while it seems necessary that we be governed by means of party, it is not necessary that we be governed for the sake of party.

Partyism as the servant of the people has its proper place; rampant partyism as the master of the people deserves to be overthrown, for it then threatens the very principles of representative government.

But how about a new third party ?

We believe that a great majority of those who care to interest themselves in political questions, are sincerely anxious to see the country well governed, and yet have not full confidence in the politicians in either camp.

Should such men unite to form a third party, and can they hope to do so with success ? Is a frequent question.

It was by such action, it is said, that the " mugwump " element of the Republican party, in 1884, recorded its disapproval of an unacceptable candidate, and taught that party that the way to victory lay only in the nomination of clean men. But the " mugwump " organization fell to pieces when President Harrison was nominated and it is doubtful, whether, as an organization, it will make itself felt in the next United States national election.

There are certain lines of fiscal policy that keep the Canadian parties apart to-day. Thinking men, when Dominion matters are under discussion, here find ample room for a divergence of opinion, and, according to their conclusions, attach themselves to the party representing one or the other of these views.

It would be necessary for a third party, in its appeal to the electorate, to rely wholly on a " purity platform," and while its influence, for a time, might be good, it would cease to have a raison d'etre, and at the same time cease to live, as soon as the old political parties put up clean candidates.

Unless it can be founded then on some fixed principles of fiscal policy other than a mere " purity platform," an independent third party, extending throughout the Dominion, seems little likely to maintain lasting organization or obtain a powerful influence.

In provincial and civic affairs, where the main—in fact the only— issue is one of an honest and economical administration, there is room for a third party ; but it is hard for men who were yesterday called Conservatives, to-day to consent to be called anything else, even where this change of name implies no change of sentiment.

There seems to be, then, at the present time, but one course open towards securing the remedy for these evils which exist in our political system, and that is, for Christian young men, working within existing party lines, to make their influence felt, and strongly felt, in favor of what is honest and honorable. But how ? How often does a young man, fired with interest and zeal, ally himself with some political organization in the hope thereby of gaining a wider knowledge on the great questions of the day, and of benefitting his generation by aiding to spread wise doctrines.

After a few evenings spent in low-ceiled halls, reeking with stale tobacco and the odor of spirituous liquor, he awakes to find to his disappointment that "important questions" occupy very little of the active politician's attention, and that unless willing to engage in the all-important pursuit of catching votes, be the means ever so dishonorable, there is no place for his activity.

The usual course taken in such a case is to quietly drop out disgusted with the whole affair, determined never again to know or care about matters political, and even to refrain from voting unless actually dragged to the polls by some personal friend.

Now, I would advocate an exactly contrary course. Nowhere are men of principle more feared and their abhorrence made more of than in these same clubs that form, we are told, the party machine. I believe that if Christian young men, banded together on principles of truth and good government, were to join these organizations, take active part in their caucuses and deliberations, and work heartily in support of honest men by honest means, they would do much towards improving the kind of men who should represent us and the methods by which they should be elected. If our political clubs have no use for such adherents, and give them to understand that they wish no dictation as to policy and methods, at election times, from "purists," then is the time for a new Conservative and a new Liberal organization to arise, composed of men attached, it is true, to opposing policies, but determined to struggle for the mastery only with honorable weapons.

But no Christian young man is safe in entering any place of political strife, unless he starts with the determination to steadfastly adhere to certain fixed principles, ready at any moment, if need be, to sacrifice all thought of personal advancement and self-interest, rather than abate one jot or tittle of the programme he has adopted. As among these principles, let me call attention to the following, that should commend themselves to the Christian sense of every young man in this community :—

1. Party cannot always be followed.

2. Corrupt methods, even when used to elect good men, are unjustifiable.

3. Public office is a public trust.

1. There are some who will tell you that party should always be followed. Where you endorse its policy and respect its representative I heartily agree. Where you are doubtful about its policy, yet have confidence in the ability and integrity of its nominee, I might also again answer, yes. Where you accept the policy, but

with reason have no confidence in the party candidate, I unhesitatingly answer, no.

If the caucus of your party disgraces itself by permitting the nomination of a man of unworthy character, then that organization does not fairly represent the real sentiment of the party, and honest men are justified in passing over such a choice, and declaring for a man whom they can respect. Their defection from the nominee of the machine, may temporarily defeat the party in that constituency ; it will eventually strengthen it, not only there, but throughout the country at large. There are times when a party's defeat may be the greatest good fortune it can fall heir to, since it may thus be enabled to slough off its old skin and emerge in purity to renewed vigor.

I am not sanguine as to the usefulness of a third independent party, but the hope of the nation lies in the independents who are not afraid to do their conscientious duty, even if the knife be used to wound that which is dear to them.

2. Next, we have the pernicious doctrine that corrupt practices are sometimes justifiable, if deemed necessary to elect a good man.

An honest man lost many votes in the recent municipal elections because he refused to pay day's wages to laborers who would, under those circumstances have remained in the city and have voted. " I have no money for that purpose, gentlemen," said he. It did not appear a very grievous sin. The men only wanted $1.50 a day, just what they would lose by remaining idle for that day, but according to the statute it was bribery, and being questionable, the candidate would not avail himself of the opportunity. The city lost the services of a good man. Some day she will awake to the consciousness that such men can ill afford to be lost.

Very specious are the arguments brought up to support this doctrine. " Your candidate will be defeated," say the managers. " A bad man will get in." " If you will only fight fire with fire, we will win, otherwise we must suffer defeat." Defeat it may appear to human eyes, but better far to spend one's days with an unsullied conscience, than occupy the Premier's chair, with the knowledge that a soul was perjured to secure it.

To show what can be done, let me cite an instance from real life.

A certain well-known political club, through the influence of Christian young men among its ranks, not long since pledged itself to support the following resolution :—

" Whereas it is an undoubted fact that the only safeguard of constitutional government lies in a pure electorate ; and

" Whereas the present campaign is distinctly understood to be one for honest, as opposed to dishonest administration ; and

" Whereas the opinion prevails in certain quarters that political clubs are willing to secure the results desired by corrupt practices ; and

" Whereas this misconception deprives this club of the desired support of many among our young men who are willing to work on pure lines to secure the return of honest men ; be it

" Resolved, that this club wish it to be plainly understood by the public, that from its inception it has been, and in future will be, strongly opposed to making use of intoxicating liquors, bribery, or " telegraphing," in order to return the candidates of its choice ; and that it will only employ such methods as are lawful, and commend themselves to the good moral sense of the community."

If a club will pass such a resolution it is deserving of success. Whether it shall secure such success and ever maintain a high standard of morality, depends very largely upon the support it shall receive from the Christian young men of this community. Unsupported by them it must either die or lower its standards to meet the popular demand.

3. Lastly, we must remember that public office is a public trust, and to the victor does not belong the spoils. The adverse workings of this principle are easily enough discernible. It leads to the distribution of public offices among " heelers " and incapables, whose only claim for recognition is that they brought in so many votes at the last election. They may be utterly incompetent, never mind, their influence, acquired generally at the tavern, is too great to admit of their claims being passed over, they must be given a snug berth somewhere, at the public expense. It is the hope of such reward that inspires much of our political " patriotism."

No Christian young man has any use for politics unless he tenders his services from a sincere desire to see the right triumph. The moment he expects other reward for his services, he lays himself open to temptations that cannot fail,—sooner or later,—to wreck his moral life.

Had we a body of Christian young men, who were willing to work only because their cause was just—who withheld their support when called upon to abate one iota the rigidness of their principles, tremendous as may seem the task, I believe they could do much towards bringing politics up to their level, provided they resolutely refused to give their assistance on any other terms.

We remember how Earl Warwick grew so great and powerful that he set up and dethroned monarchs at his will. As " kingmaker," he was greater than the king himself. In a county north of the St. Lawrence, not many miles from Montreal, once lived a man who could elect or defeat any candidate either party might put forth. Often was he asked to allow himself to be returned to

Parliament. His answer was always : " No, by compelling you to nominate upright men, I serve my country better as a simple citizen, than I could do within the halls of Ottawa."

That man was the " kingmaker" of the country. Would it not seem that the united Christian sentiment of Montreal might do for this city what one man did for an entire district. And has not the world a right to expect that Christianity and Christian young men will do something to rescue the national life from the perils into which it at times shall have fallen ? Great has been the service in ages past, that Christianity has rendered to politics.

To-day, Roman law is regarded as the basis of modern jurisprudence. In the time of the later republic and the early empire, Roman law and Roman philosophy may be said to have reached their perfection, yet, no greater contrast has ever existed before the eyes of the whole world, than that between the grandeur of the Roman law and the debased life of the Roman people. But when Christianity entered the Roman world, the Imperial law found an ally in Christian ethics, which it had never had during the reign of paganism, and discovered, too, a higher sanction for its precepts than mere economic interests. From the time of Constantine onward, the influence of Christianity on Roman law is remarkable, and always on the side of morality in the highest sense of the term.

Do you realize that it was Christianity that gave to the world those two great factors in civil liberty—a consolidated public opinion and an efficient system of representative government ? Constantine was the first Roman Emperor, yes, he may be characterized as the first monarch of olden times, who ruled with " public opinion at his back," and since his day, though whispering at times, this voice has never been wholly silenced.

The early church method, too, of electing its officers was the first purely Democratic system of government, and the tie that bound together the churches in all the provinces of the Empire and extended to many in even barbaric lands, was the first successful attempt at true federation. So strong was this tie of union, that it postponed not for years, but for centuries, the downfall of the Roman Empire.

Is the mission of Christianity as a purifier of politics ended ? Having given to the world such mighty principles, should she be content to stand idly by, while they are abused ; or has she a duty to perform in seeing that they are preserved and safeguarded ? Surely the necessity for action exists. The precedent is undeniable.

Why then, any hesitation ? " I speak to you young men because ye are strong." I cannot doubt your willingness to act, the difficulty must lie in the knowing how to go about it. To meet this end then, let me offer a few suggestions by way of peroration.

1. There is a public opinion : It is asleep perhaps, but it is not dead. My belief is that we do not half know or value this power. Everyone of us is a factor in forming and arousing it. As Christian young men then, we have a plain duty before us in agitating in season and out of season, for purity in elections, honesty in administration, and genuine statesmanship in policy.

2. But you may thunder on in denunciation of iniquity in high places until you are gray, without disturbing the repose of the corrupt politician, if you neglect to secure and use your vote. This is a weapon of self-defence placed in your hands that you can ill afford to let idly hang unused within its scabbard. If you are old enough and qualified to become a voter, let not another month go by without claiming what is both your duty and privilege, and having claimed it, use it as a Christian man.

3. Then I would suggest that each one honestly attempt to inform himself with regard to matters of national import. If you cannot watch and sift all the contradictory reports of the daily press, you can at least purchase and read a few such books as Dr. Bourinot's "Constitutional History of Canada," and learn how this country came to be acquired by your forefathers, and under what general laws we live together in unity.

4. This leads me to a word of caution and entreaty. We are here a mixed people. Among us are differing languages, religions and ancestry. Naturally it is difficult for one portion of the community to fully understand and appreciate the merits of the other. We must cultivate agreement where agreement is possible, and genuine toleration where agreement is impossible. The confederation is only as strong as its weakest link. That weakest link is undoubtedly Quebec, and it remains for us here to prove that the two peoples can live in harmony, and that out of this union can spring one nation. Let us brand as a traitor that man who, for personal ends, undertakes to stir up hatred and hostility, a civil war of hearts, among the differing classes of a community that God intended should dwell together in unity.

5. Finally, let us cultivate a spirit of faith and buoyant hope in the future of this our native land, and in the great work of nation building. God grant that each one of us, to whatever part of the task he may be appointed, may faithfully and conscientiously do his duty.